DRUM SET WARM-UPS

Essential Exercises for Improving Technique

Rod Morgenstein

Edited by Rick Mattingly

Berklee Media

Associate Vice President: Dave Kusek
Director of Content: Debbie Cavalier
Business Manager: Linda Chady Chase
Technology Manager: Mike Serio
Marketing Manager, Berkleemusic: Barry Kelly
Senior Designer: David Ehlers

Berklee Press

Senior Writer/Editor: Jonathan Feist
Writer/Editor: Susan Gedutis
Production Manager: Shawn Girsberger
Marketing Manager, Berklee Press: Jennifer Rassler
Product Marketing Manager: David Goldberg

ISBN 978-0-634-00965-5

1140 Boylston Street
Boston, MA 02215-3693 USA
(617) 747-2146

Visit Berklee Press Online at
www.berkleepress.com

DISTRIBUTED BY

HAL•LEONARD®
CORPORATION
7777 W. BLUEMOUND RD. P.O. BOX 13819
MILWAUKEE, WISCONSIN 53213

Visit Hal Leonard Online at
www.halleonard.com

INTRODUCTION

After years of warming up exclusively on a practice pad before tearing into my drums, I was struck by the grand realization that playing the drum set involves a dramatically wider range of body motions, movements, and coordination than a drum pad. Of course, there is no substitute for a drum pad warm-up, as it is the definitive way to focus on hand, wrist, and finger development. But what about the arm and body motions involved in moving from drum to drum, hand to foot, or reaching for a cymbal some distance away?

It was in this moment of realization that the idea for *Drum Set Warm-Ups* was born — not to mention the fact that the drum set is perhaps the only musical instrument on which warm-ups do not occur on the actual instrument itself. Imagine a guitarist or keyboardist warming up exclusively on a slab of wood!

Consider this book a natural extension of your snare/pad warm-up book(s) and use it in much the same way. Pick a page and play each exercise until it sounds and feels comfortable. String two or more examples together to create two-, four-, and eight-bar phrases. Some exercises are straightforward and relatively easy to play, while others are quite challenging. So, if a particular exercise is too difficult, move on to the next one and come back to the more difficult one at another time, or in the case of a multi-limb exercise, leave off one of the parts (for example, a quarter-note bass drum or hi-hat foot part). It is not imperative to go through the book in chronological page order, although it is suggested, initially, to go through the book this way.

Be more musical and less mechanical by varying the dynamic levels and tempos of the exercises. Most of the exercises are not intended to be applied note for note as cool fills or beats. In fact, some may seem downright unusual or even unmusical. Rather, they have been designed as drum set warm-ups to limber up the entire body (not just the wrists, hands, and fingers) and improve specific areas of drum set playing such as speed, power, control, dexterity, coordination, independence, accuracy, endurance, and agility.

These exercises were designed primarily as patterns of movement. Some will be immediately obvious, but with others, you may have to play them for a while before the pattern reveals itself. By having the arms and body moving in clockwise, counter-clockwise, up, down, side-to-side, crossover, cross-under, and crisscross motions, a greater facility and command of the drum set will be achieved, along with a dramatic increase in confidence.

NOTATION KEY

These exercises are written for a standard 5-piece drum set, but with a little imagination they can be adapted to larger or smaller kits.

Bass Drum	Snare Drum	Cross-Stick	Stick Shot*	Large Tom	Medium Tom	Small Tom	Hi-Hat	Open Hi-Hat	Hi-Hat Pedal	Hi-Hat Splash	Ride Cymbal	Cymbal Bell	Crash Cymbal

R = Right Hand   L = Left Hand   **R** = Right-Hand Crossover   **L** = Left-Hand Crossover   B = Both Hands
* Strike left stick with right stick while left stick rests on drumhead in cross-stick position

CONTENTS

A high level of accuracy can be achieved by focusing on one limb at a time. Play each exercise several times through with just the right hand and then just the left hand. Strive for an even, consistent sound, and try to strike each drum in the center. Exercises 15 and 16 are especially challenging due to the long reach from the hi-hat to the ride cymbal.

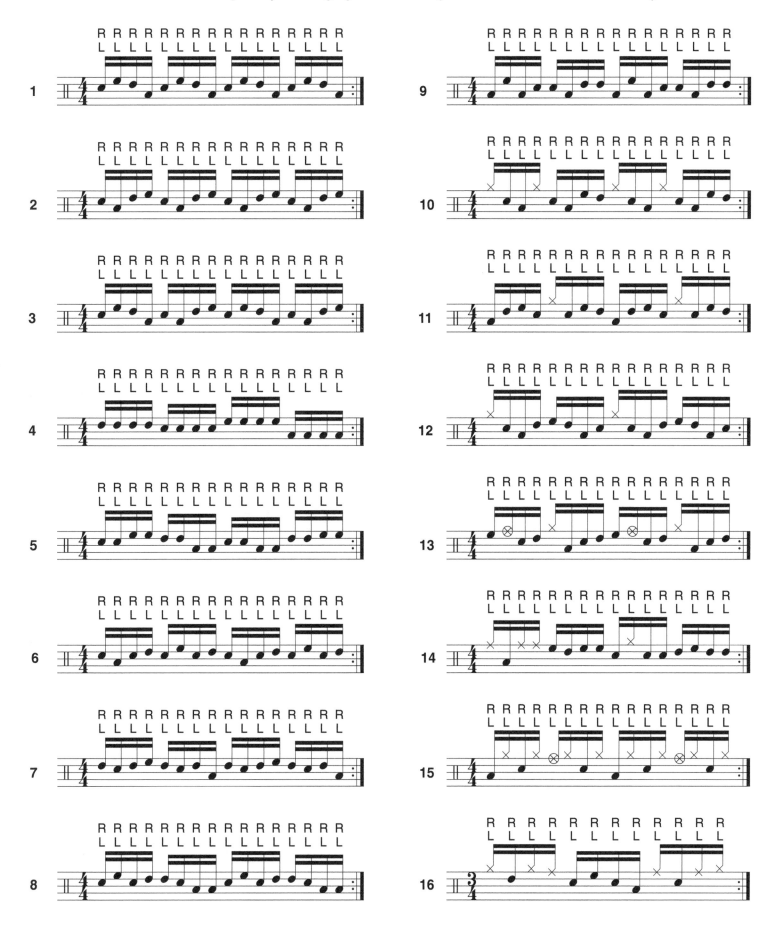

In the following exercises, one hand either repeats what the other hand plays or moves in a "mirror" image.

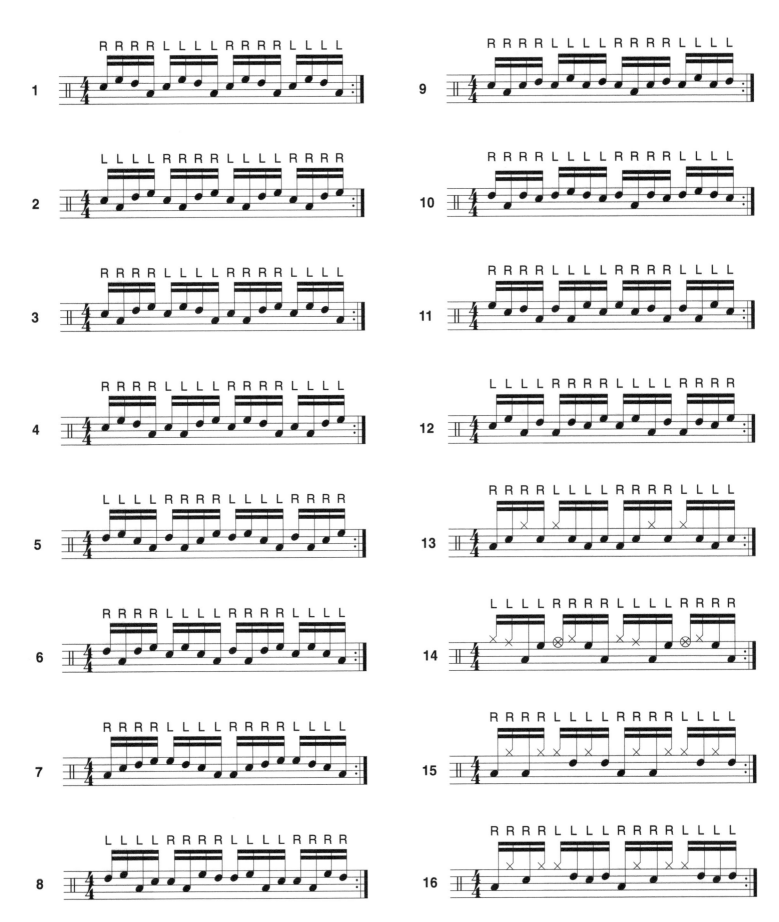

The following pages contain a variety of exercises played with alternating single strokes, with the hands moving in a variety of directions (clockwise, counterclockwise, horizontal, vertical, crisscross, or combinations). Some of the exercises might sound somewhat routine, but the idea is to force the hands, arms, and body to move in every possible direction to increase one's command of the drum set.

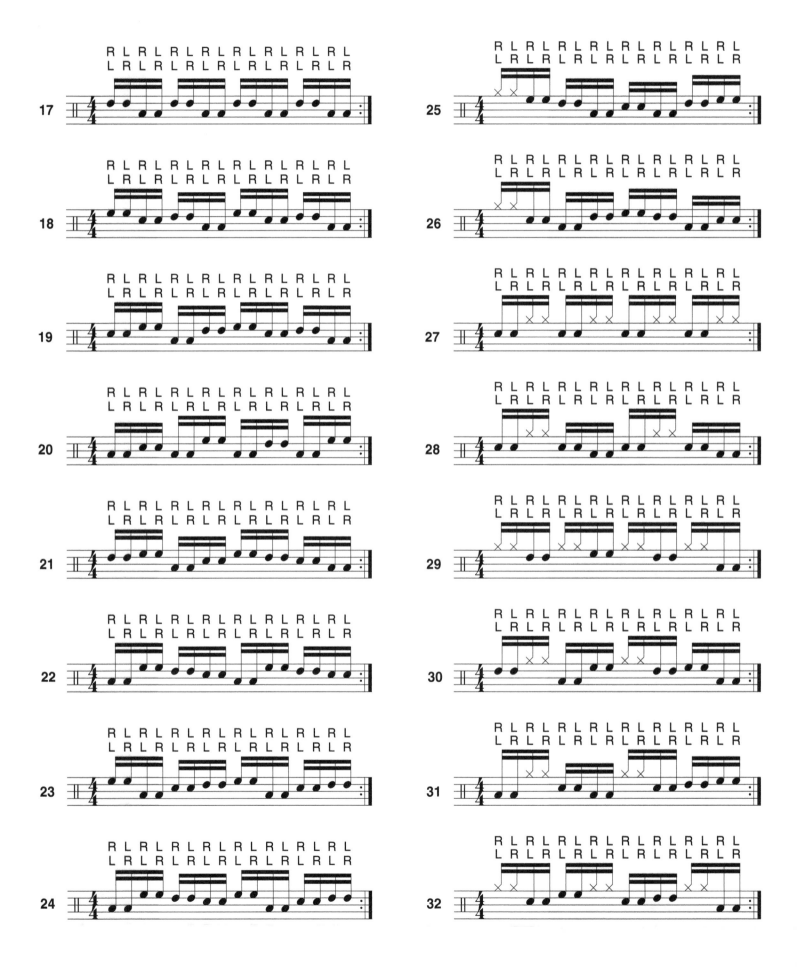

Although Exercise 33 is notated on the small tom, this single-stroke roll should be played on all the different drums and cymbals in your drum set because each surface has a very different feel.

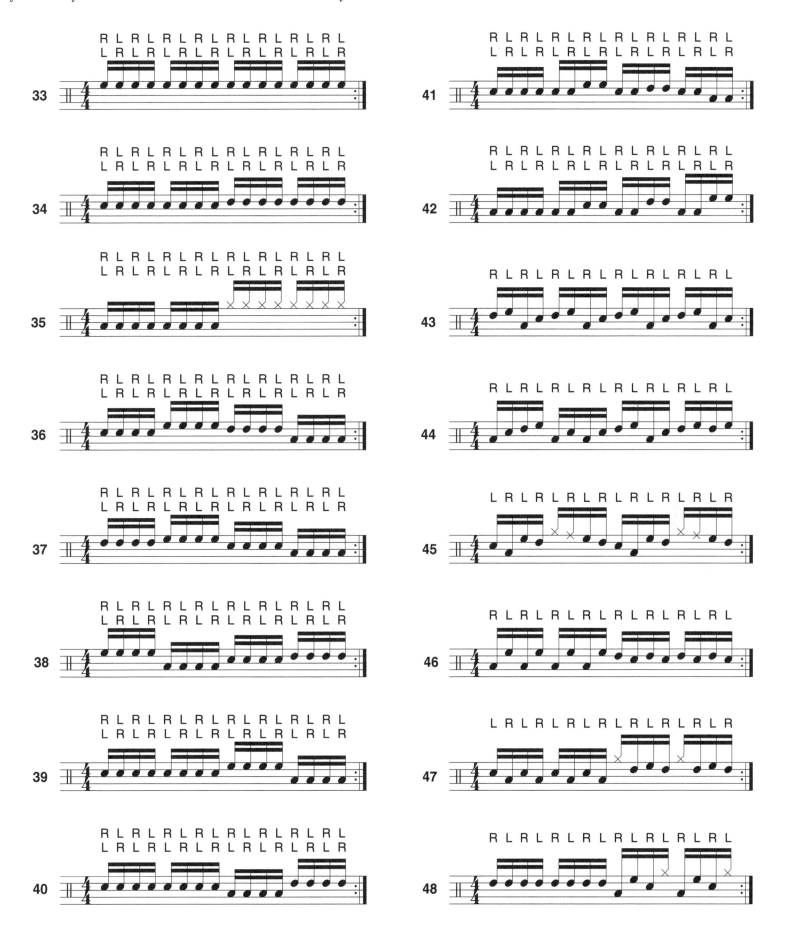

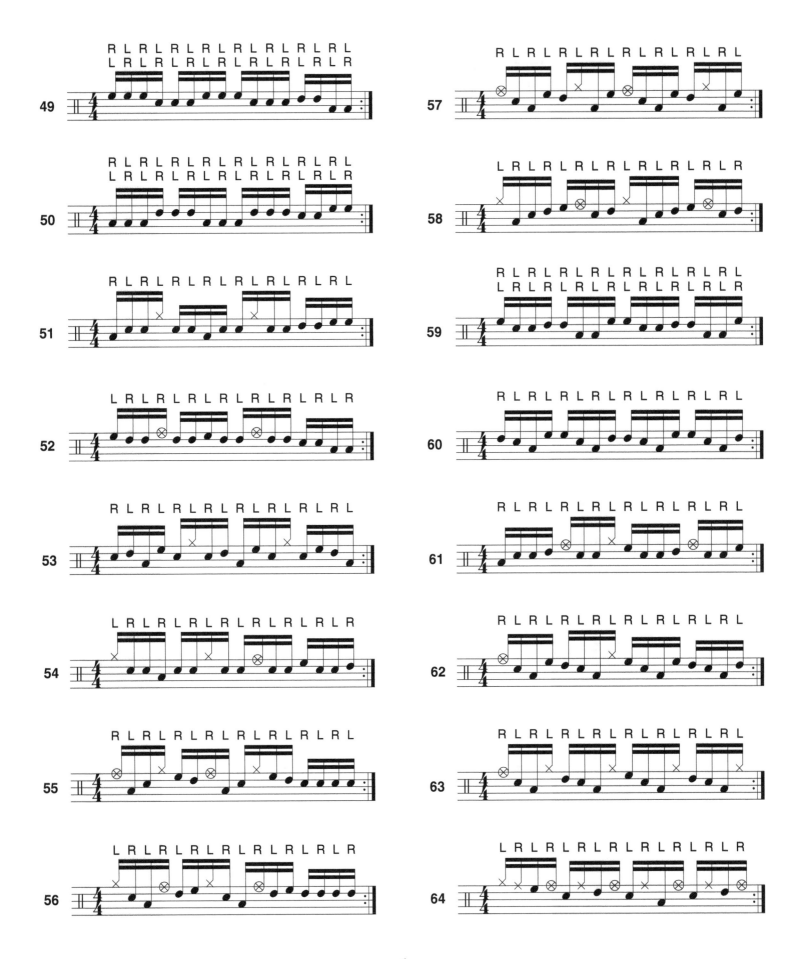

Double strokes should have an even sound. Some exercises will require a crossover to facilitate the stickings. It is tricky (and somewhat uncommon) to play double strokes with one stroke per surface, as in Exercises 17–32. Go for a smooth, fluid sound.

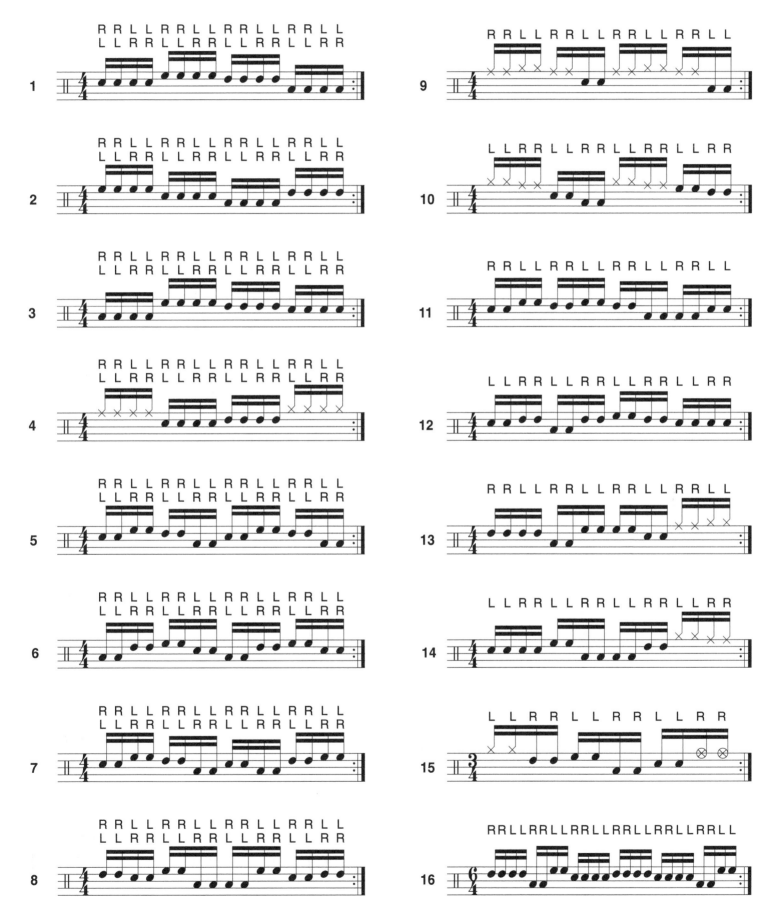

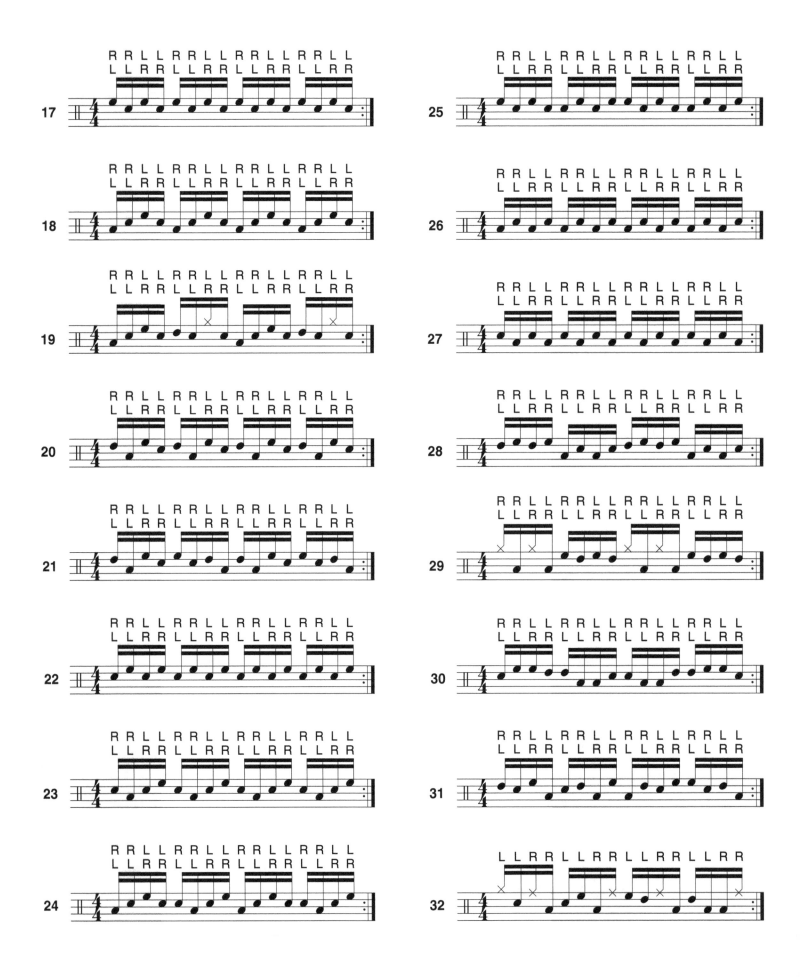

Paradiddles can be of tremendous value on the drum set. Most of these exercises apply this rudiment in non-traditional ways. Stress the first note of each paradiddle in Exercises 7–10.

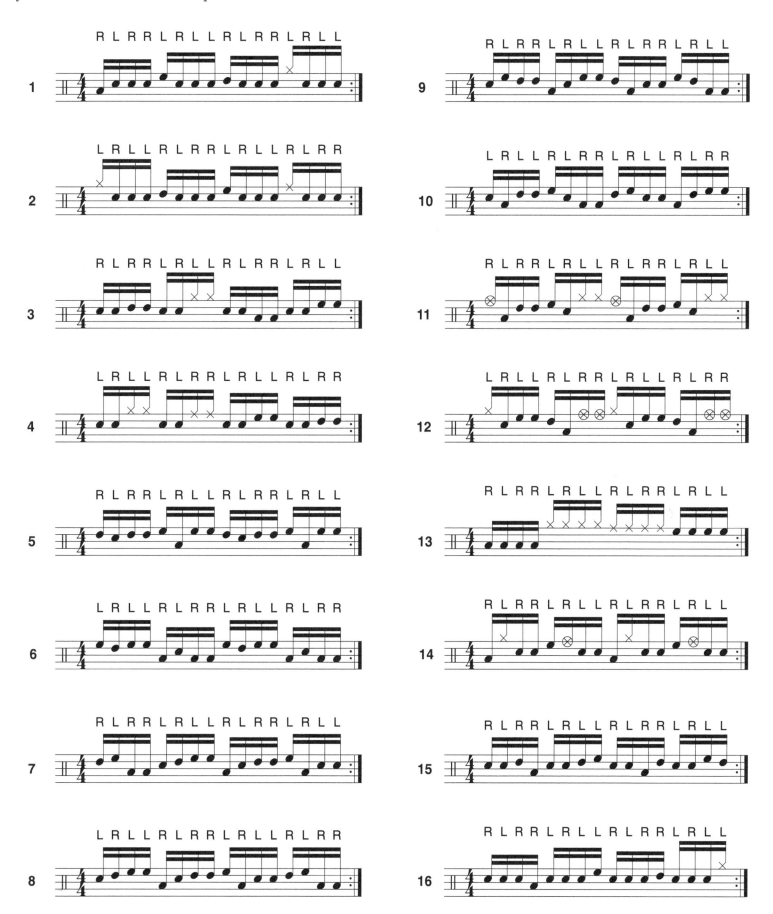

Strive for a consistent sound so that all of the stickings sound like a single hand playing continuous sixteenth notes.

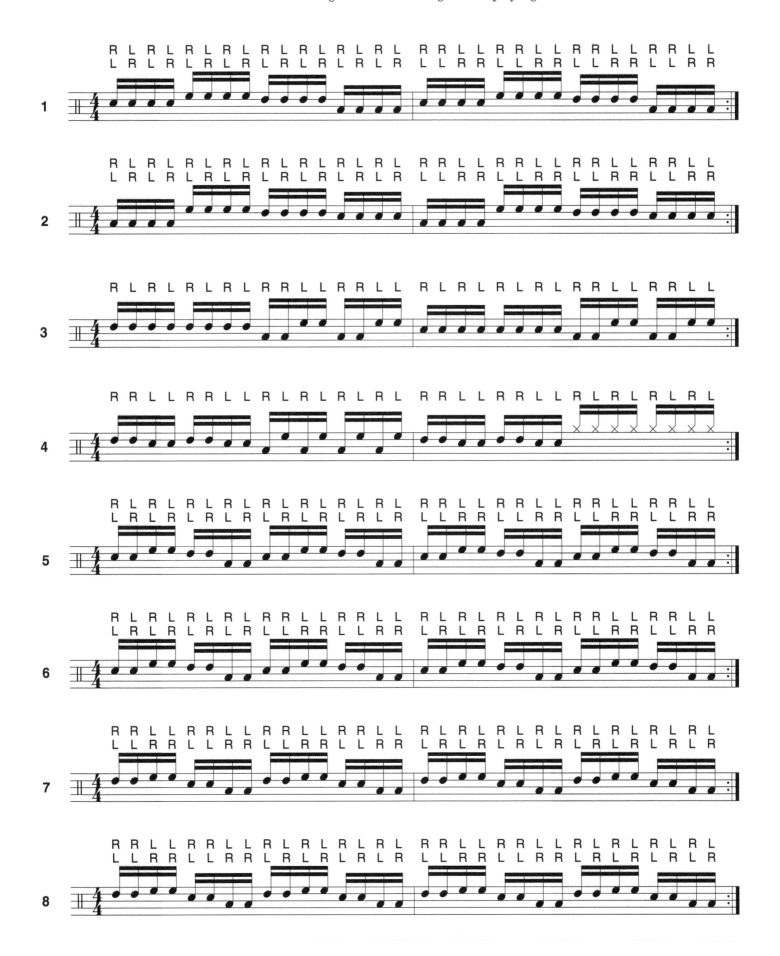

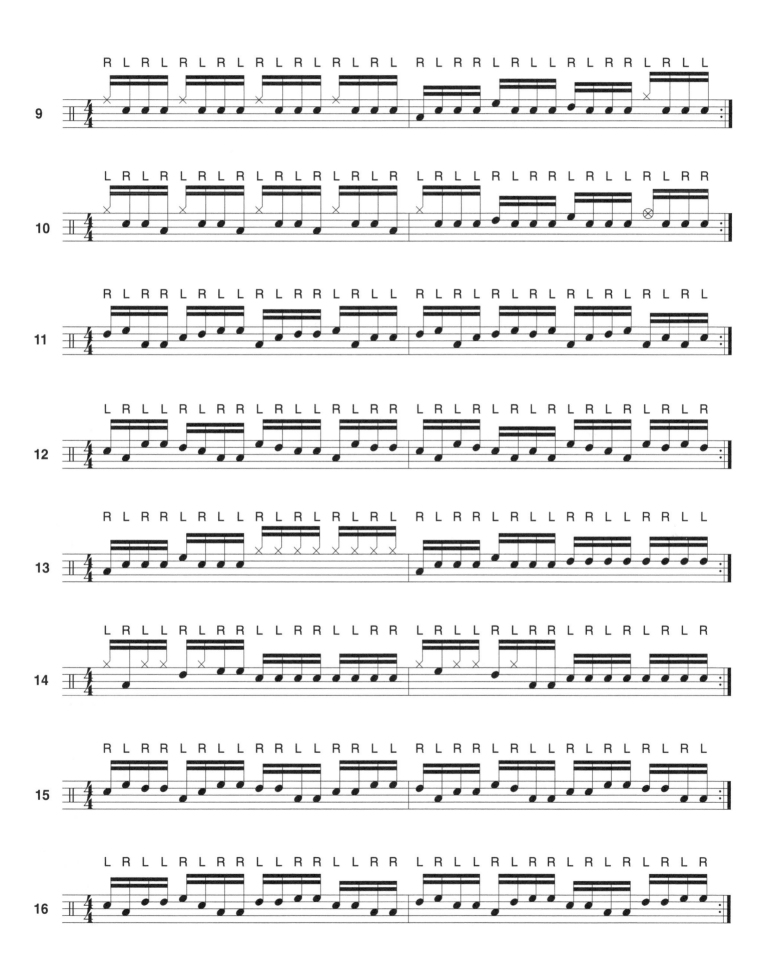

Use the hi-hat or bass drum quarter-note pattern to help define the pulse of the rhythms below.

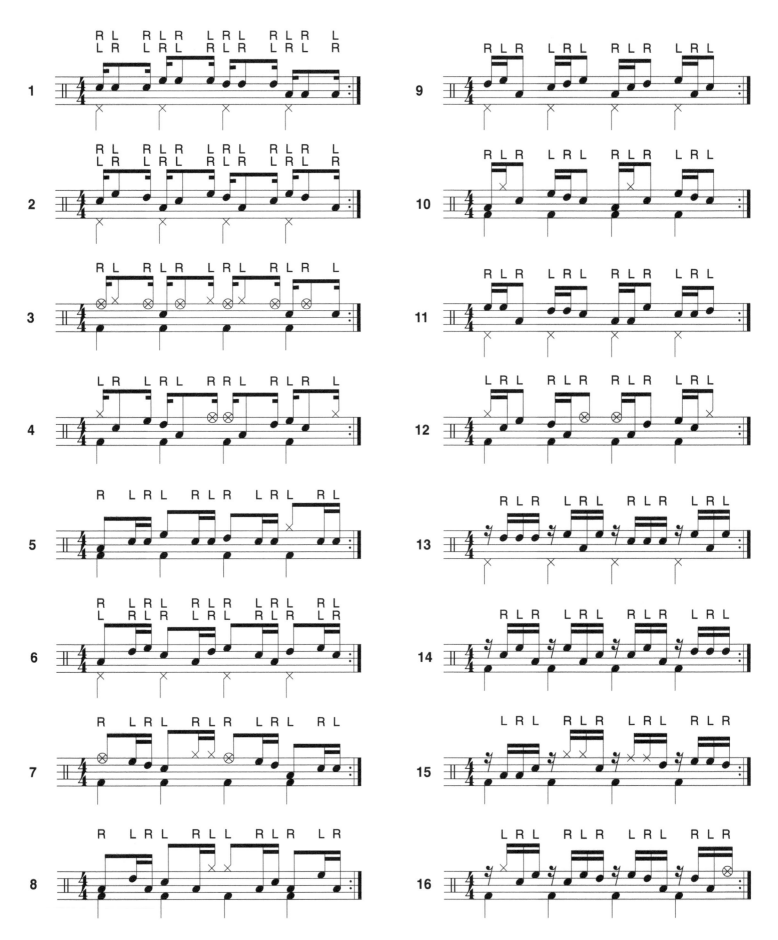

LESSON 8

SUBJECT
One-Hand Triplets

TECHNIQUE
All strokes played with the same hand

It is a good idea to play quarter notes on the hi-hat or bass drum to help define the pulse, especially on Exercises 13 and 14.

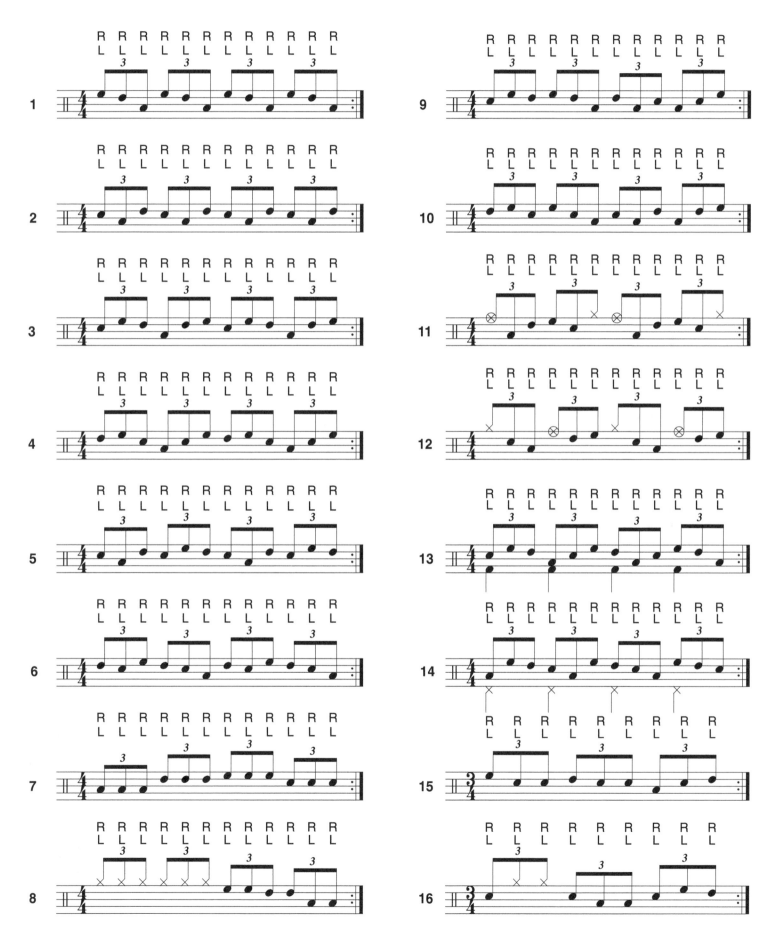

In the following exercises, one hand either repeats what the other hand plays or moves in a "mirror" image. Exercises 5, 6, 9, and 10 each involve a crossover, indicated by the sticking appearing in **bold** type.

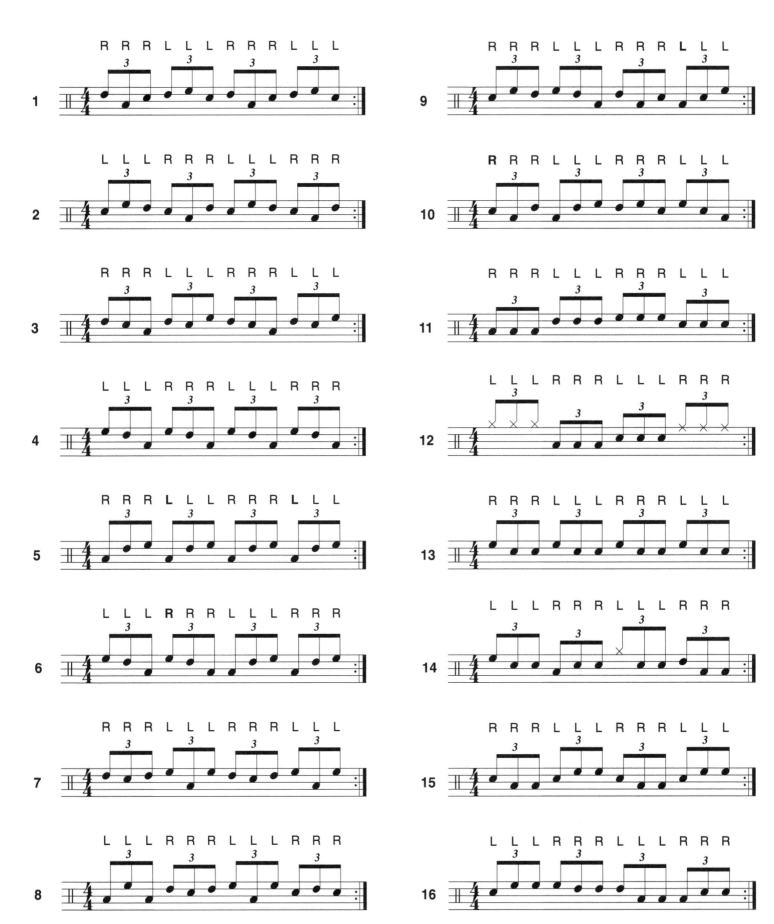

The following pages contain a variety of exercises played with alternating single strokes, with the hands moving in a variety of directions. It is a good idea to maintain quarter notes on the bass drum or hi-hat to define the pulse, especially in Exercises 33–48 and 53–56, where you are playing two notes per surface. Some exercises involve crossovers, indicated by the sticking appearing in **bold** type.

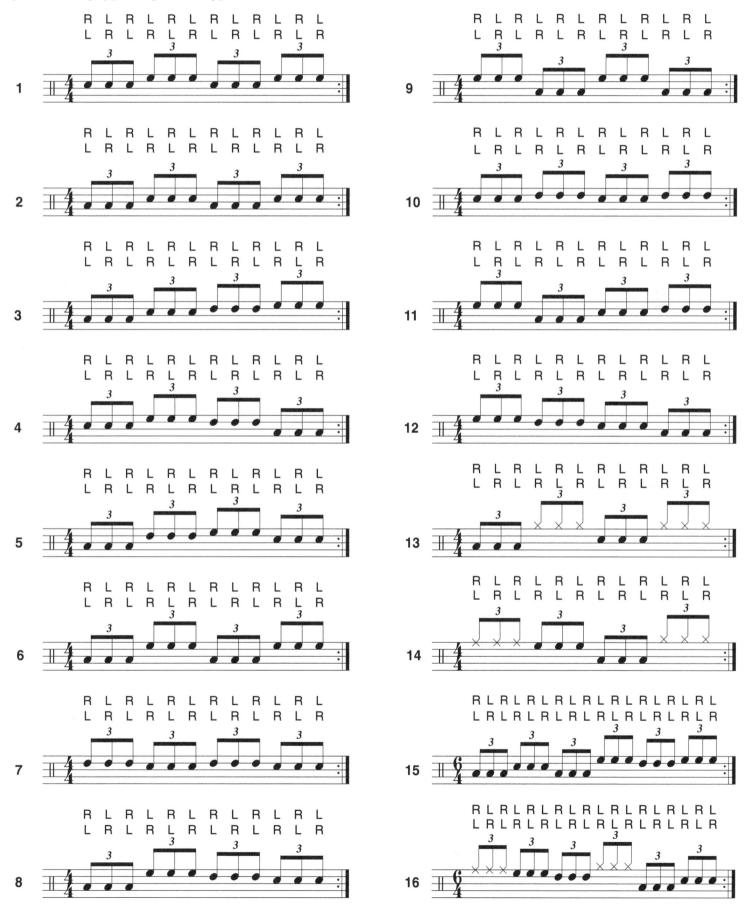

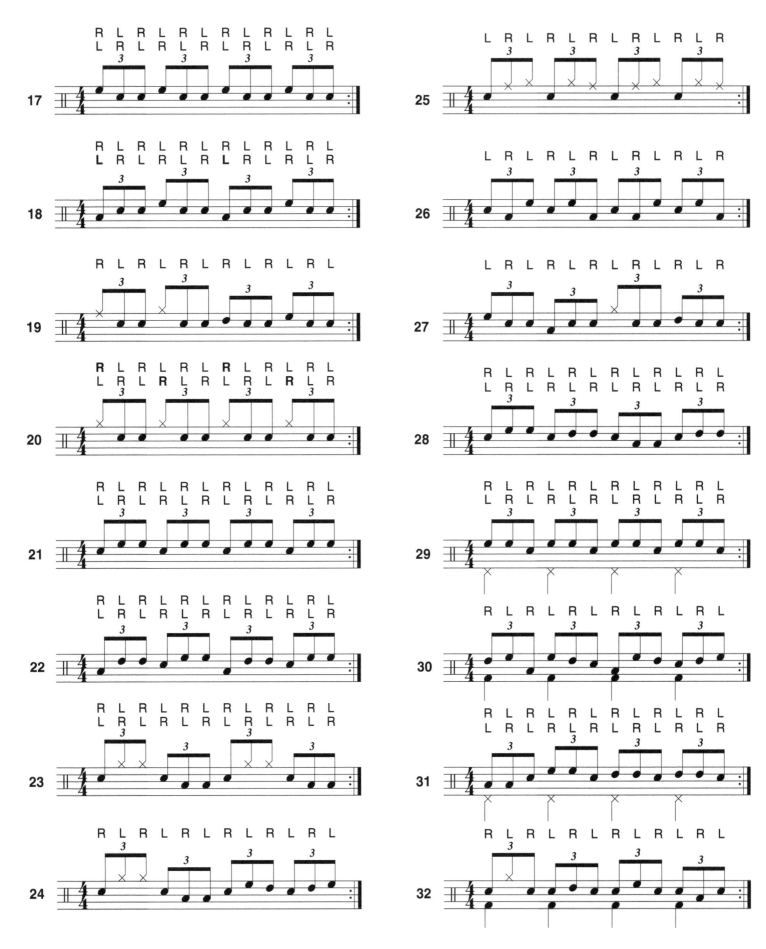

16

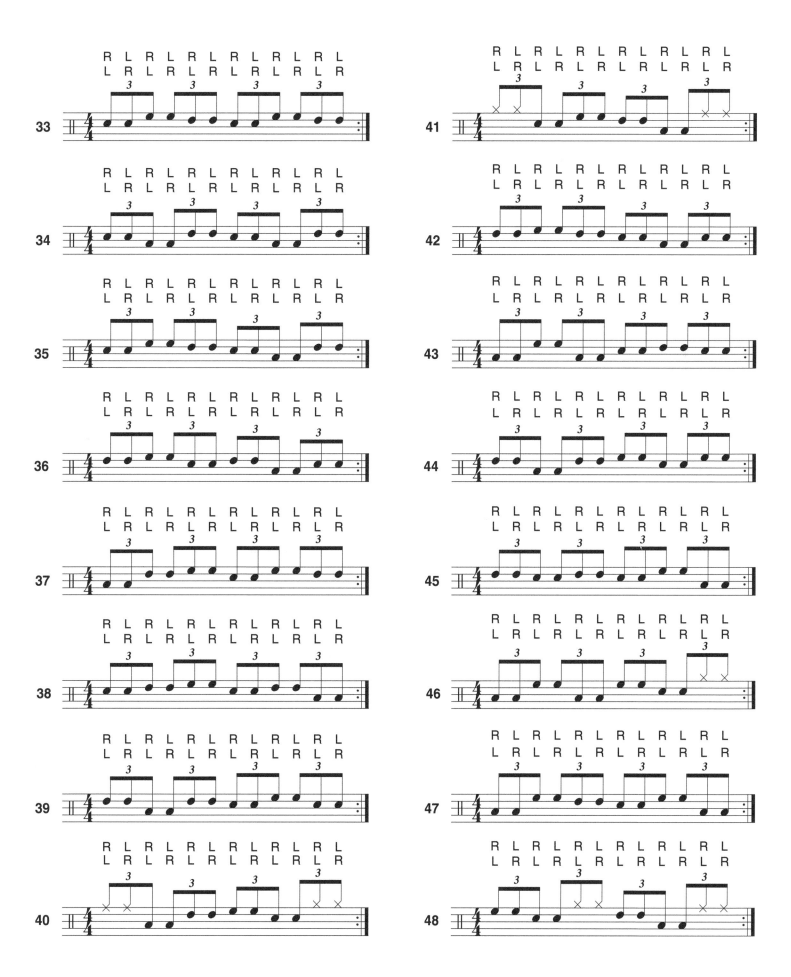

Although Exercise 49 is notated on the hi-hat, this single-stroke roll should be played on all the different drums and cymbals in your drum set because each surface has a very different feel.

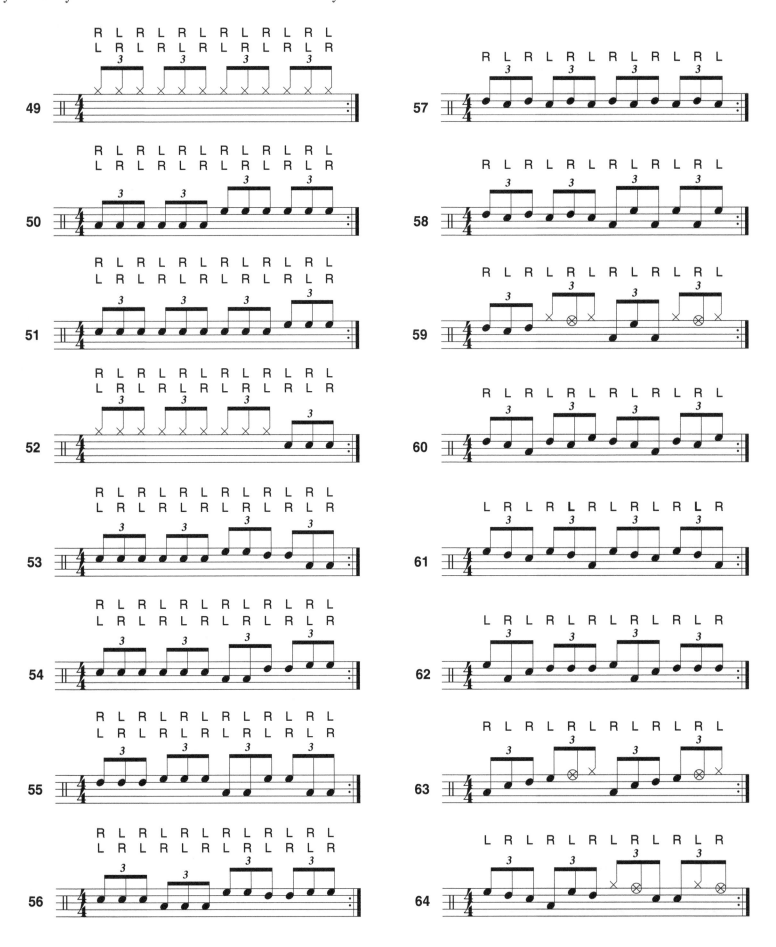

The following exercises combine one, two, and three strokes per surface. Keeping a quarter-note pulse with bass drum or hi-hat is recommended, especially in Exercise 9, where the pattern in measure two implies a three-against-four polyrhythm.

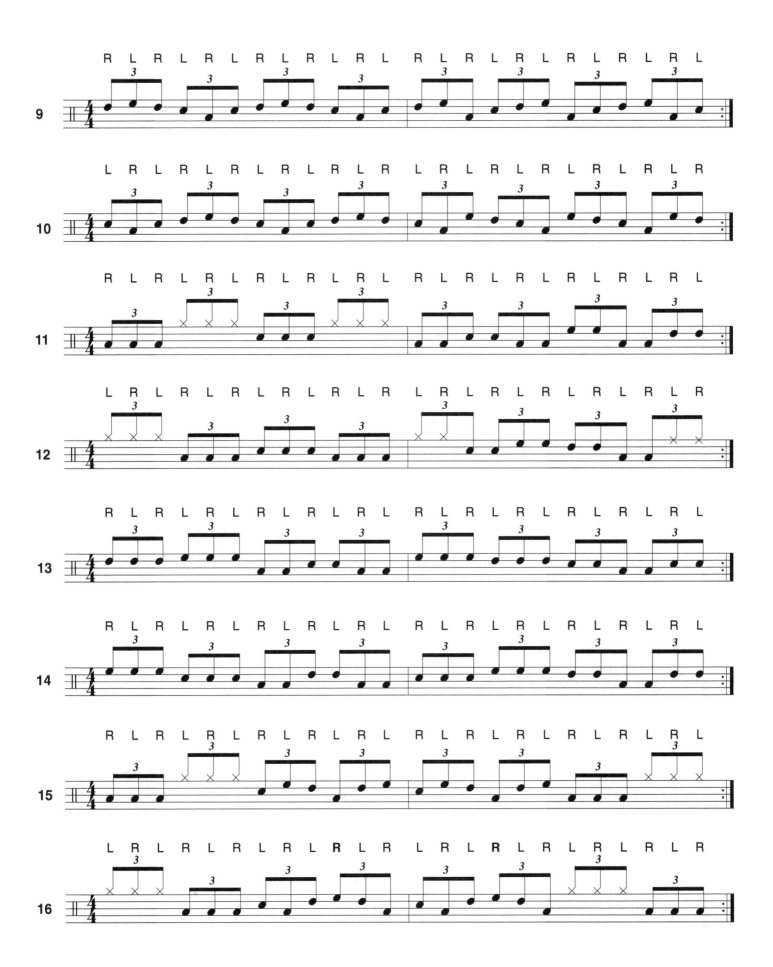

LESSON 12

SUBJECT
Triplets with Mixed Stickings

STICKINGS

RRL	RLL	RLRRLR
LLR	LRR	LRLLRL

These exercises combine single and double strokes in various combinations that are popular and useful when playing triplets.

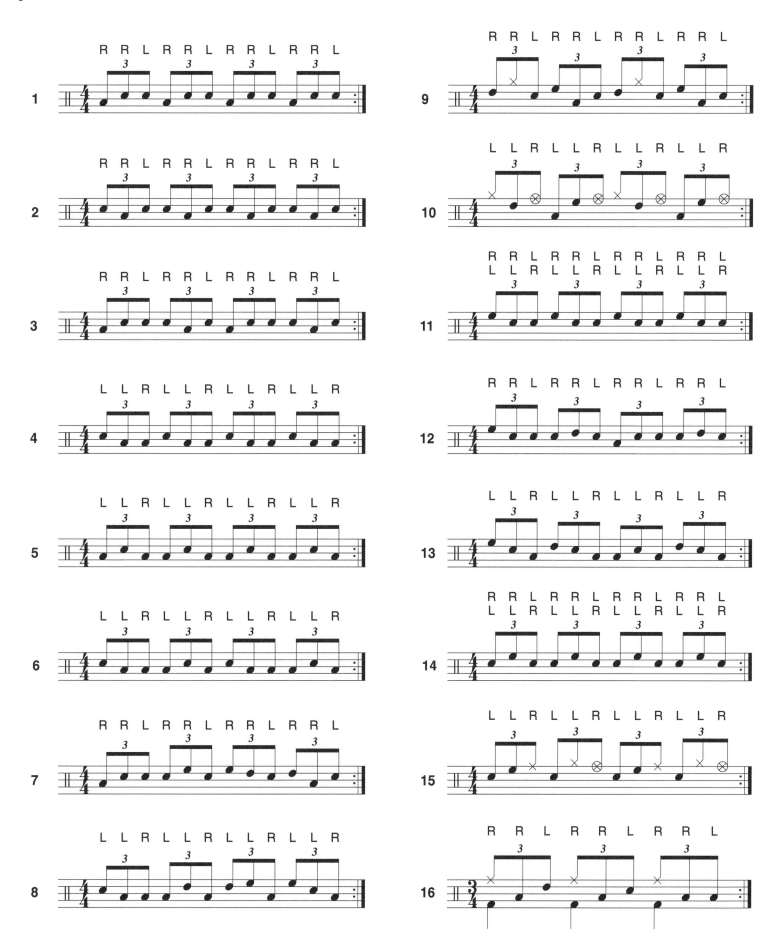

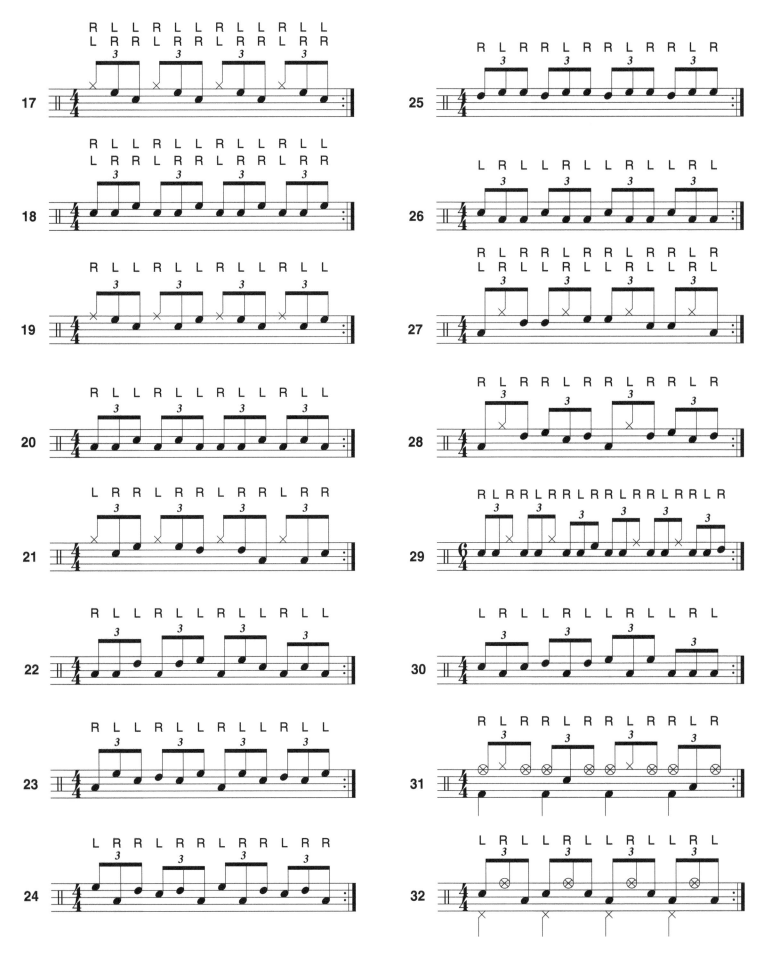

These exercises keep the arms in constant motion. Exercises 5, 6, 10, and 12 involve crossovers, indicated by the sticking appearing in **bold** type.

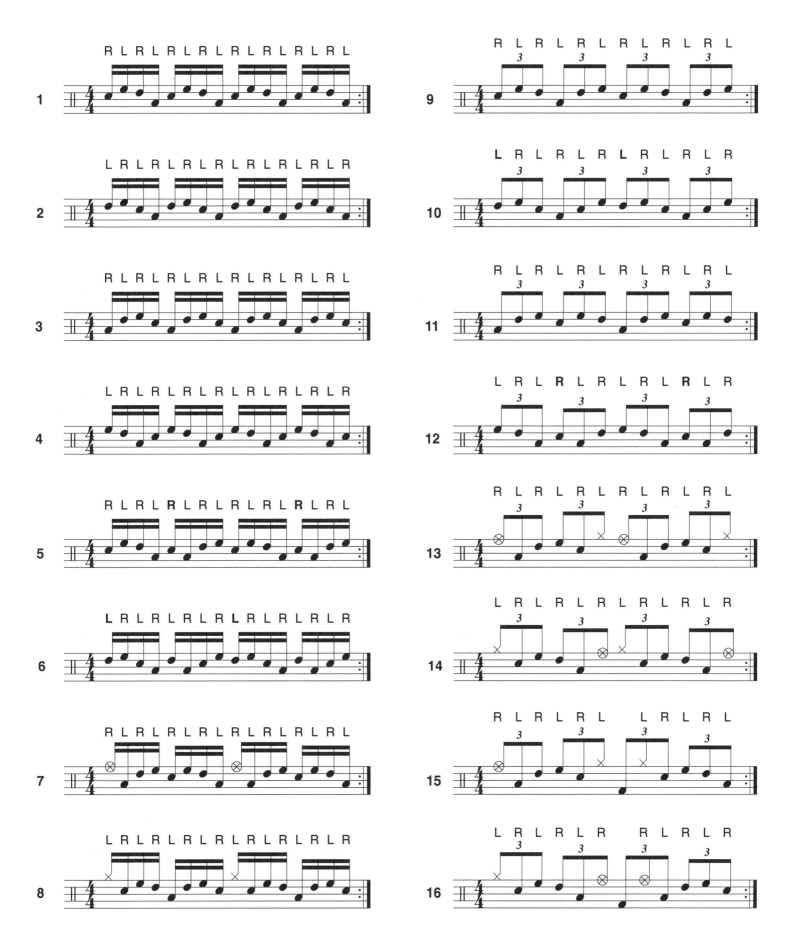

23

Note the right-hand crossover in Exercise 2 on beat 3.

25

SUBJECT
Bass Drum and Hi-Hat Endurance

TECHNIQUE
Straight sixteenths and triplets on bass drum and hi-hat pedal

This chapter contains strength, coordination, and endurance-building exercises for the bass drum and hi-hat pedal.
Although the hand patterns are written on the snare drum line, they can be played many different ways, including both hands together on different surfaces. At first, you can omit the quarter-note pulse on the hi-hat or bass drum if that is too difficult.

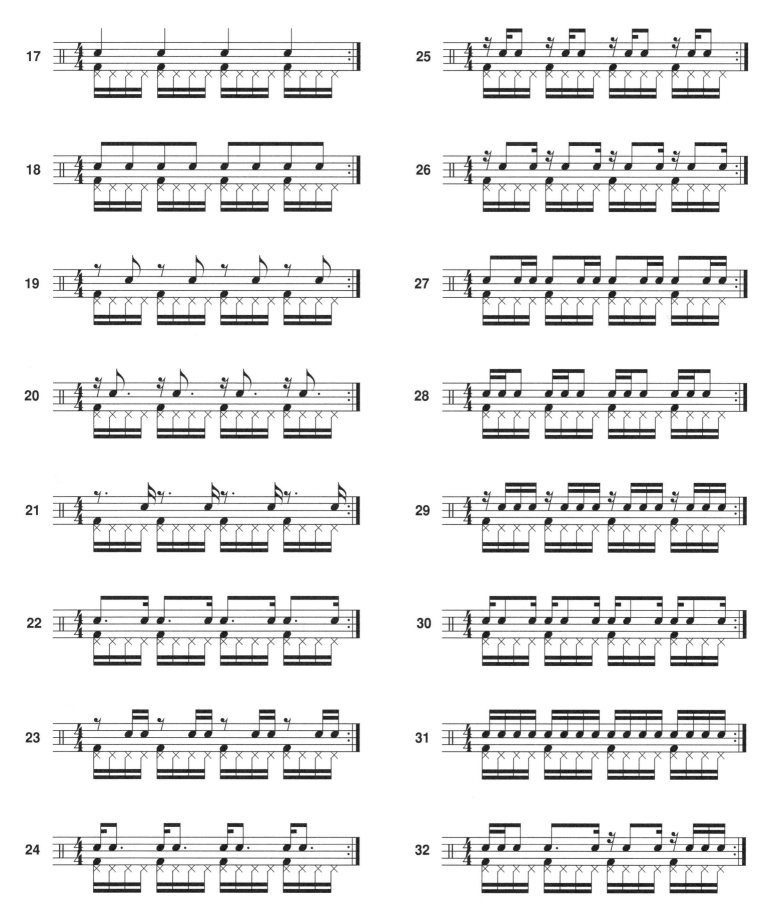

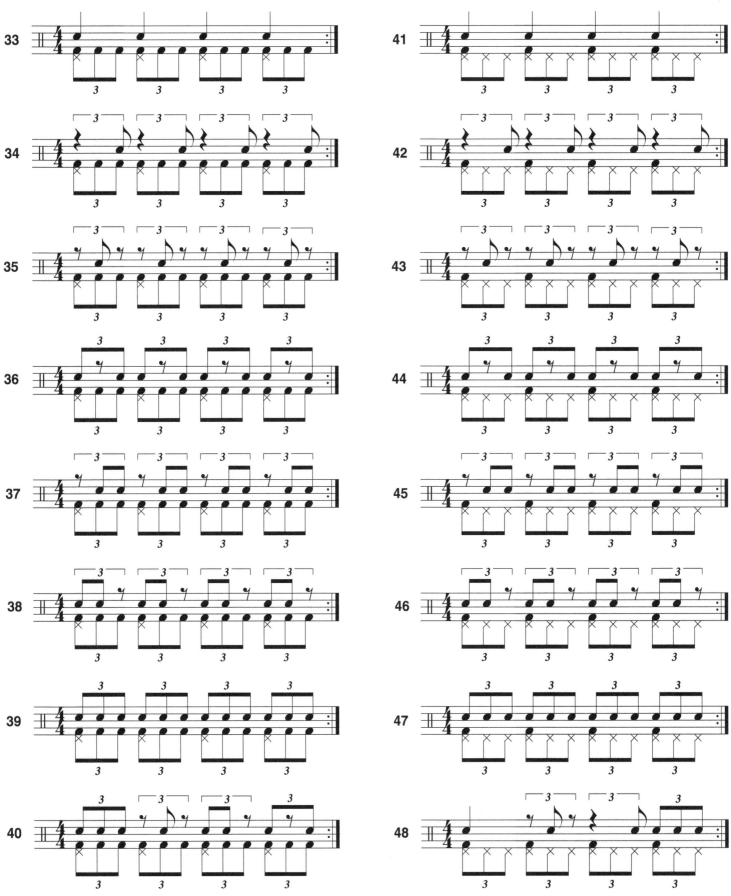

LESSON
17

SUBJECT
Alternating Feet

TECHNIQUE
Singles, doubles, and Paradiddle variations between the bass drum
and hi-hat pedal

This chapter contains a variety of patterns played between the bass drum and hi-hat pedal. Double bass players can substitute the second bass drum for the hi-hat. On each page, apply the stickings shown in the first exercise to all of the exercises. You can leave out the notated accents at first, but ultimately they help define the underlying pulse.

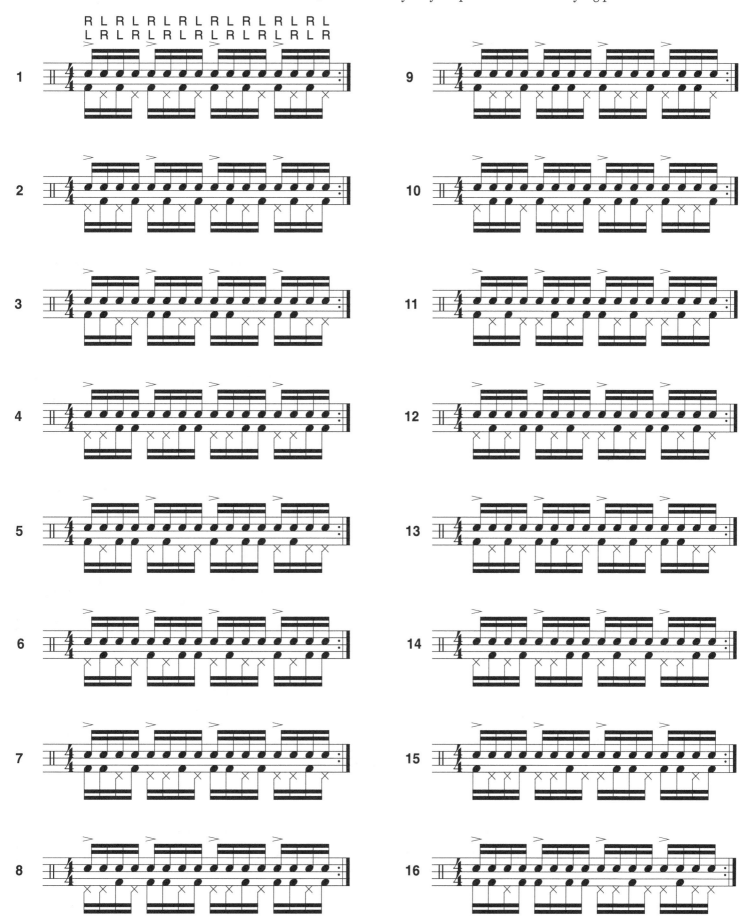

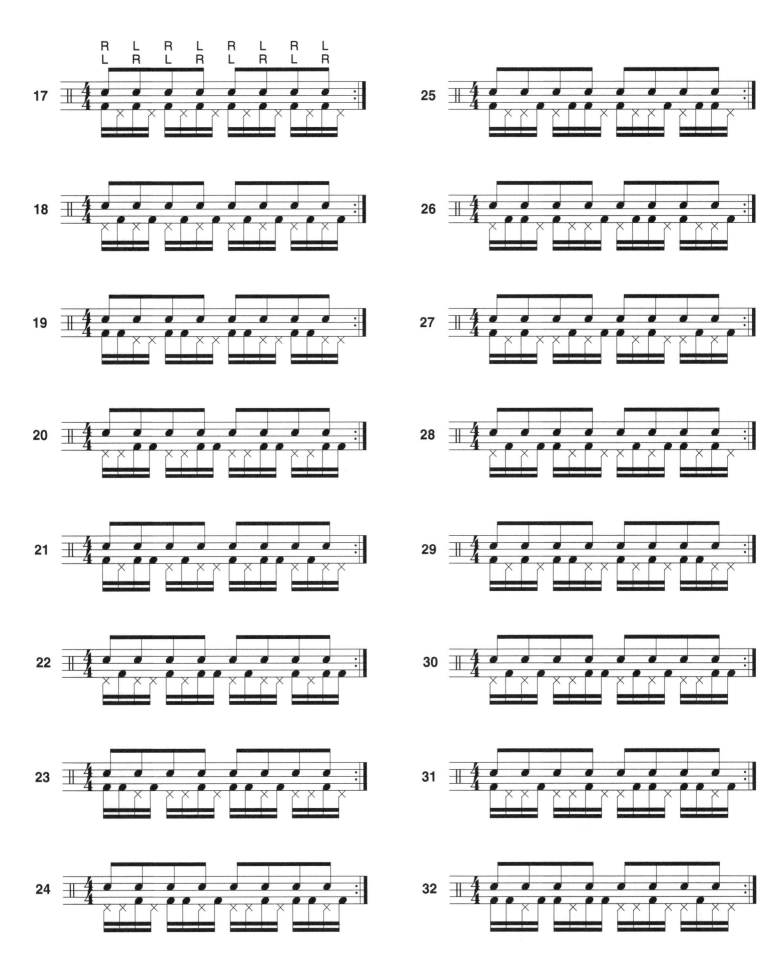

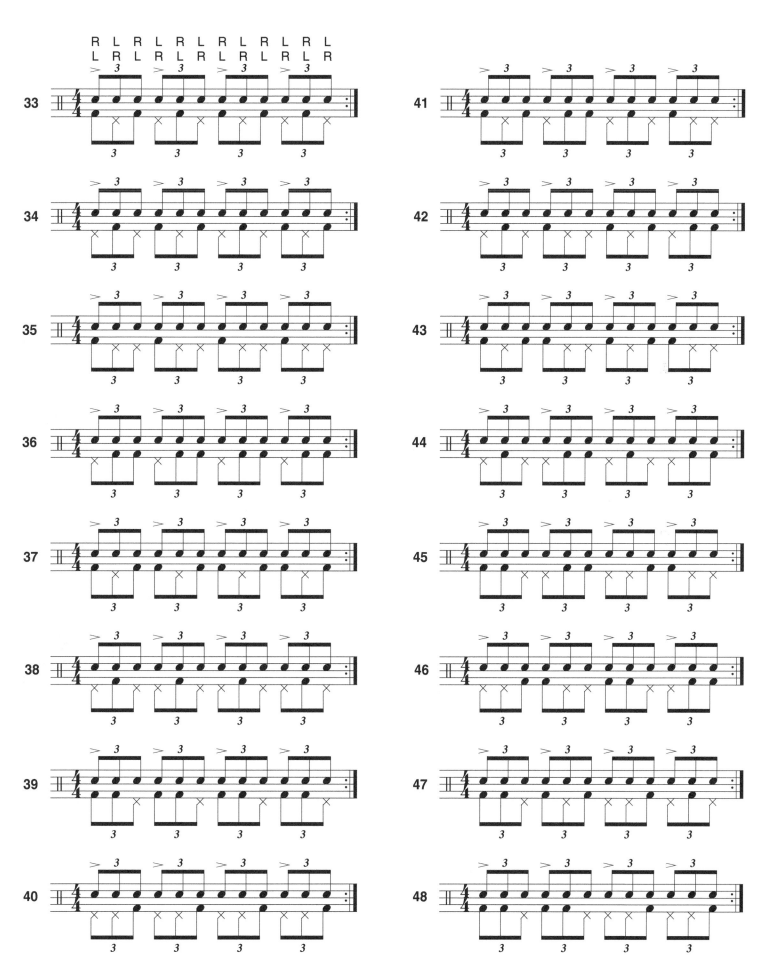

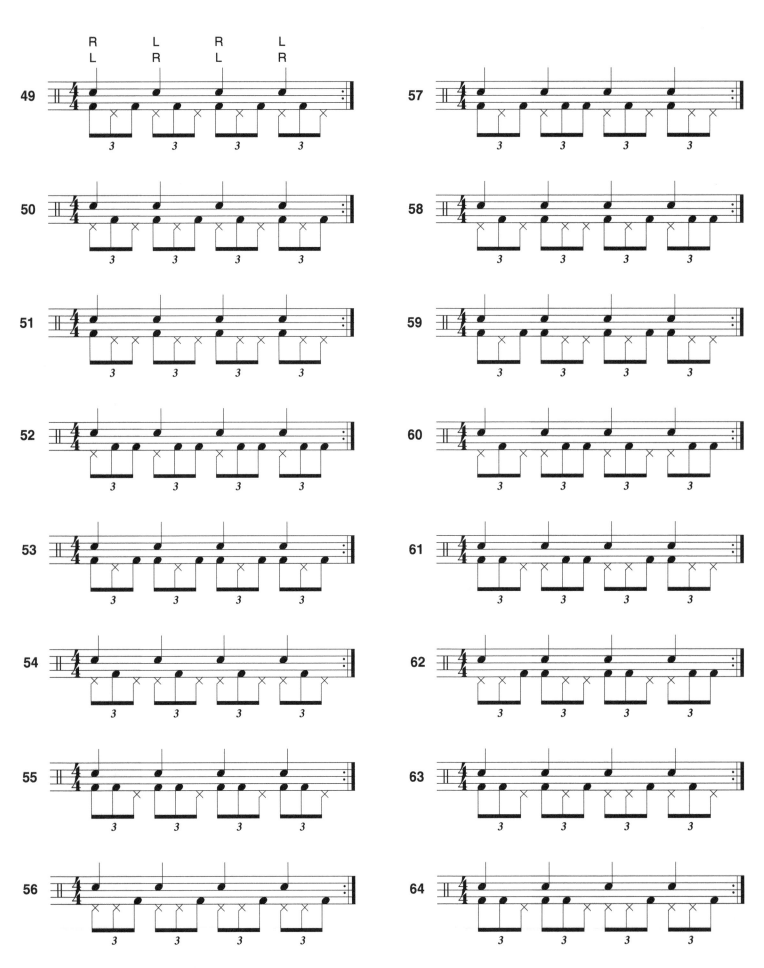

Each of the bass drum and hi-hat pedal figures on the following four pages is to be played with the four accompanying hand patterns listed above, each of which should be played for several measures in order to establish a convincing groove. Accenting the downbeat of each quarter note will help make the bass drum/hi-hat notes sound equal in volume and intensity.

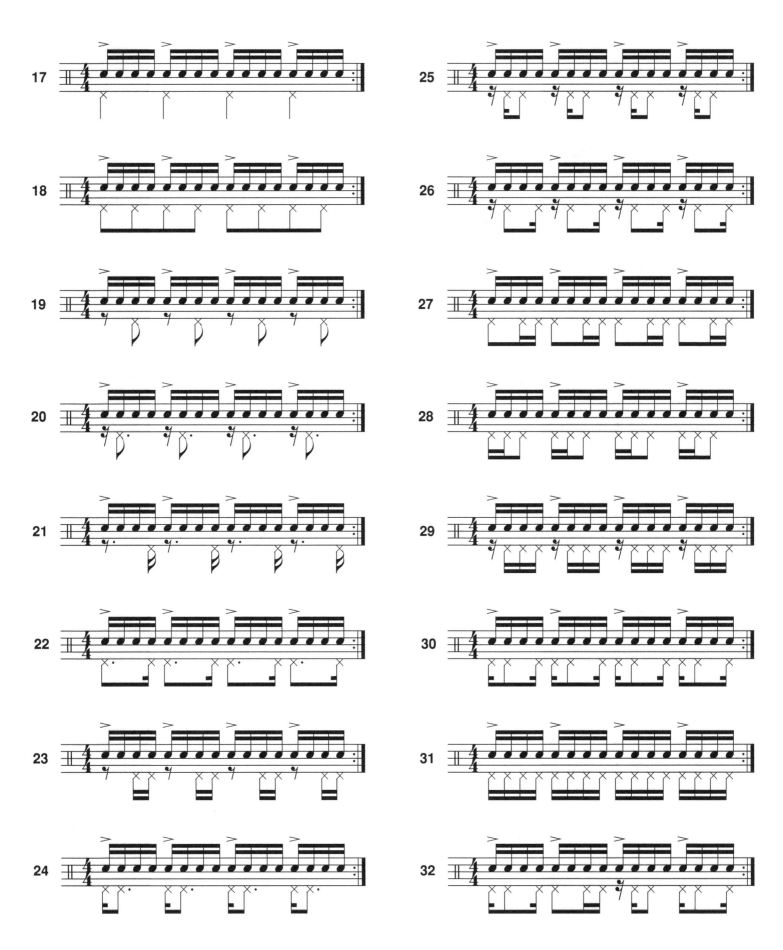

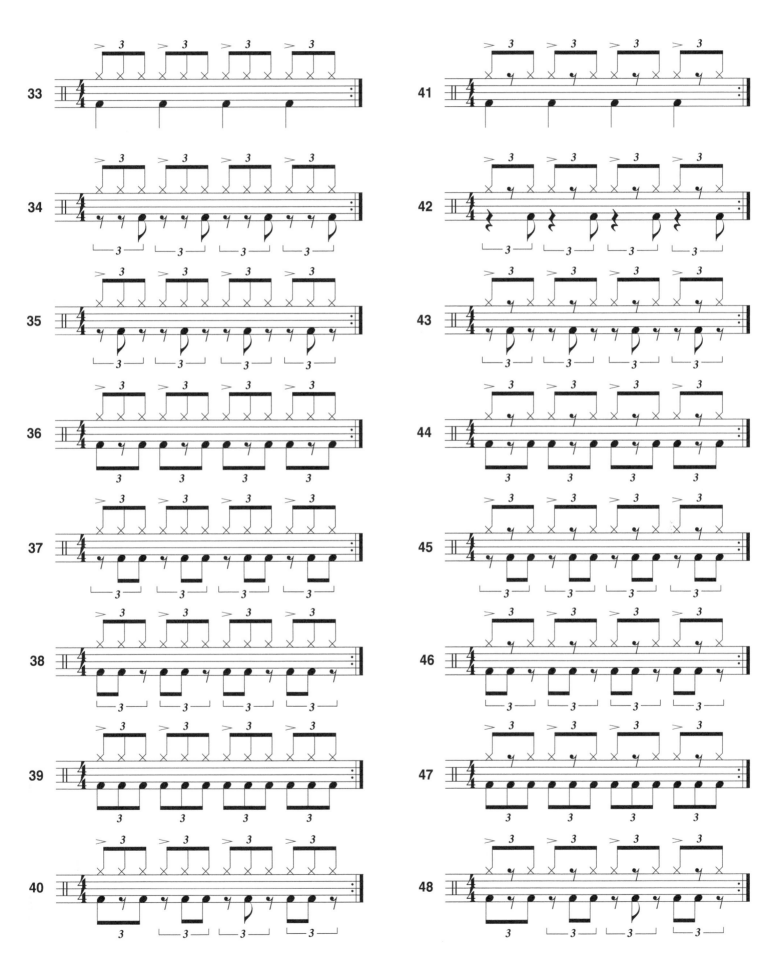

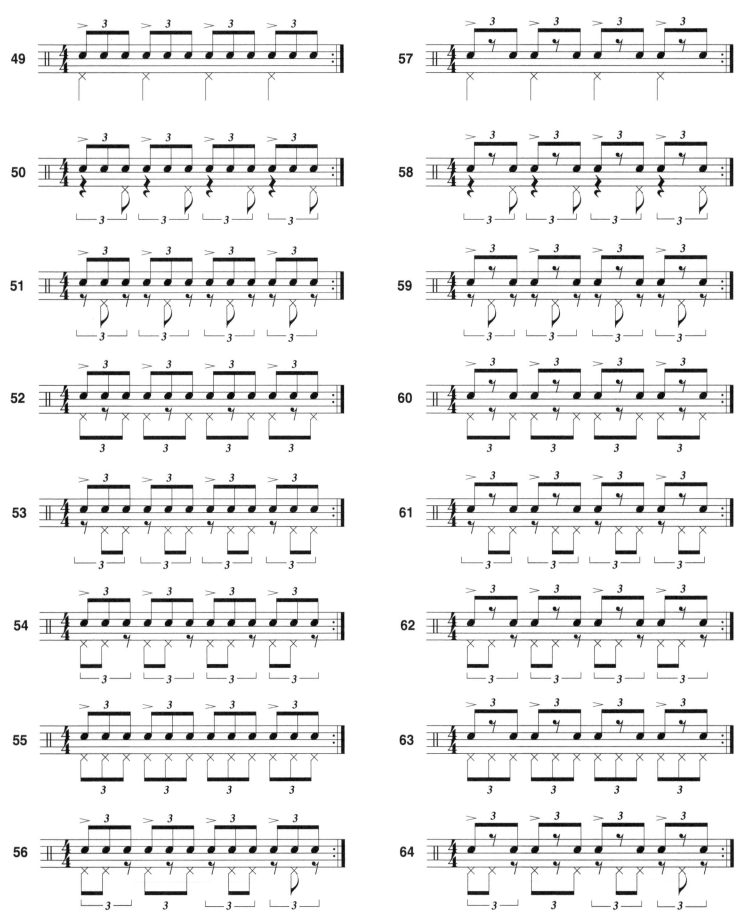

Pay attention to the specified sticking, as it changes from measure to measure. The hand part is written on the snare line but can be played on different sound surfaces or played with both hands together on the same or different drums (for example, right hand on floor tom and left hand on snare). To gain further independence and control, play quarter notes with the hi-hat foot in Exercises 1, 3, 9, and 11, and quarter notes on the bass drum in Exercises 2, 4, 10, and 12. If you have a double bass pedal, substitute the left bass for the hi-hat in Exercises 8, 15, and 16 (or on any of the examples that use hi-hat pedal).

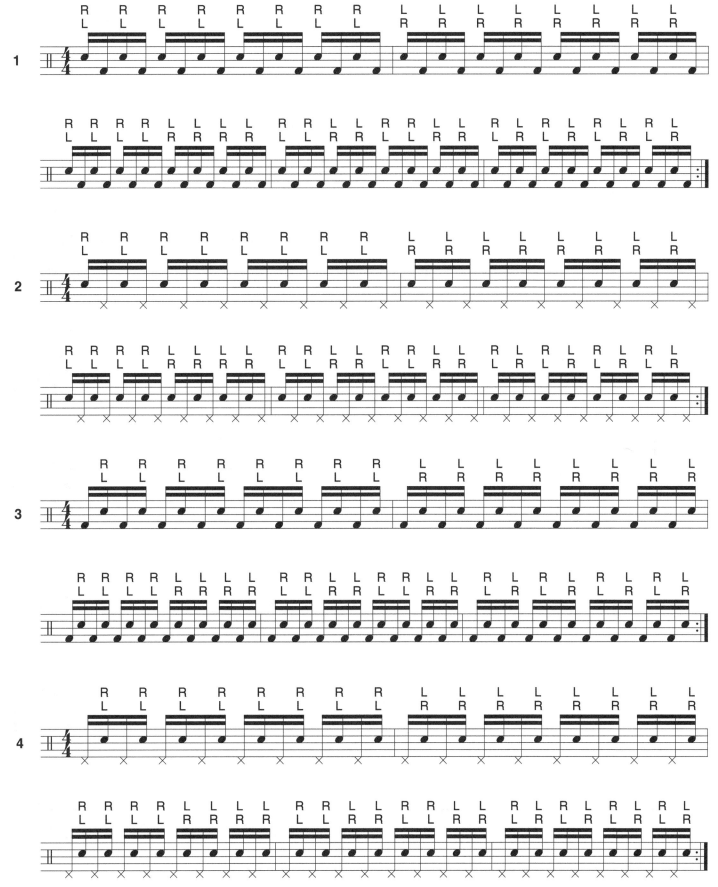

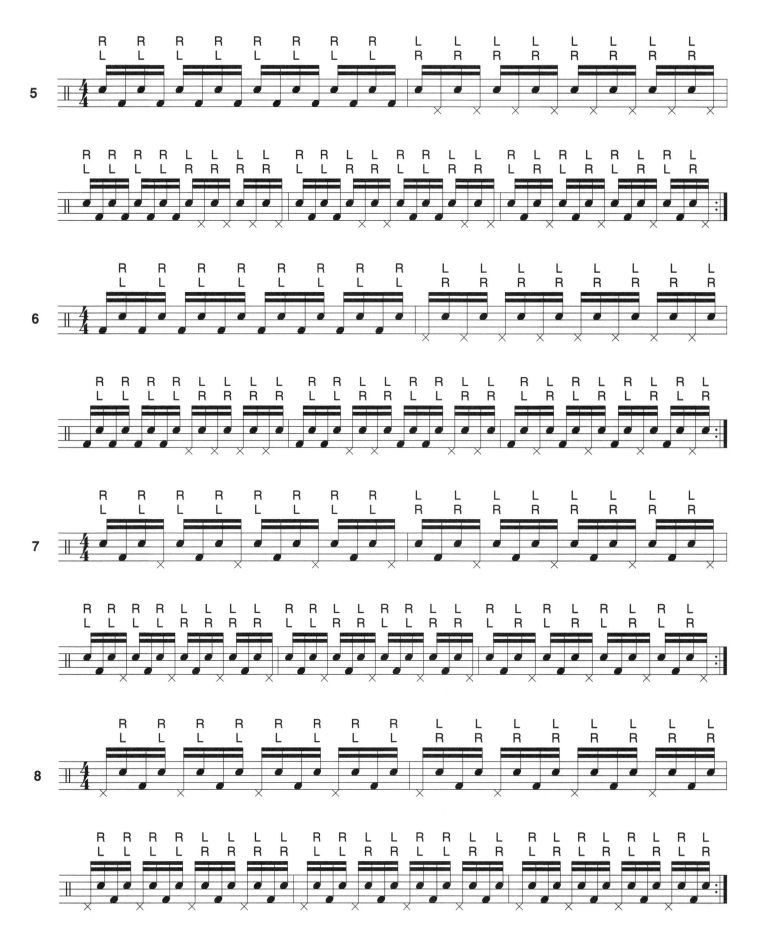

It is especially helpful to count the dotted-quarter-note pulse (1, 2, 3, 4) out loud when playing the exercises on this page so that you feel the patterns in 12/8.

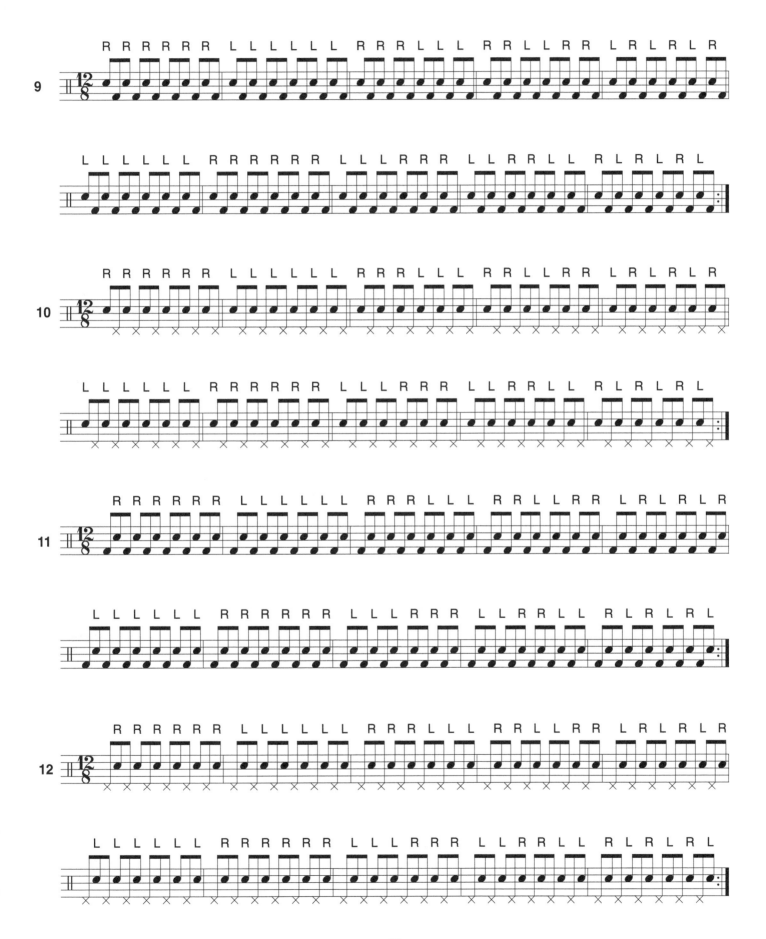

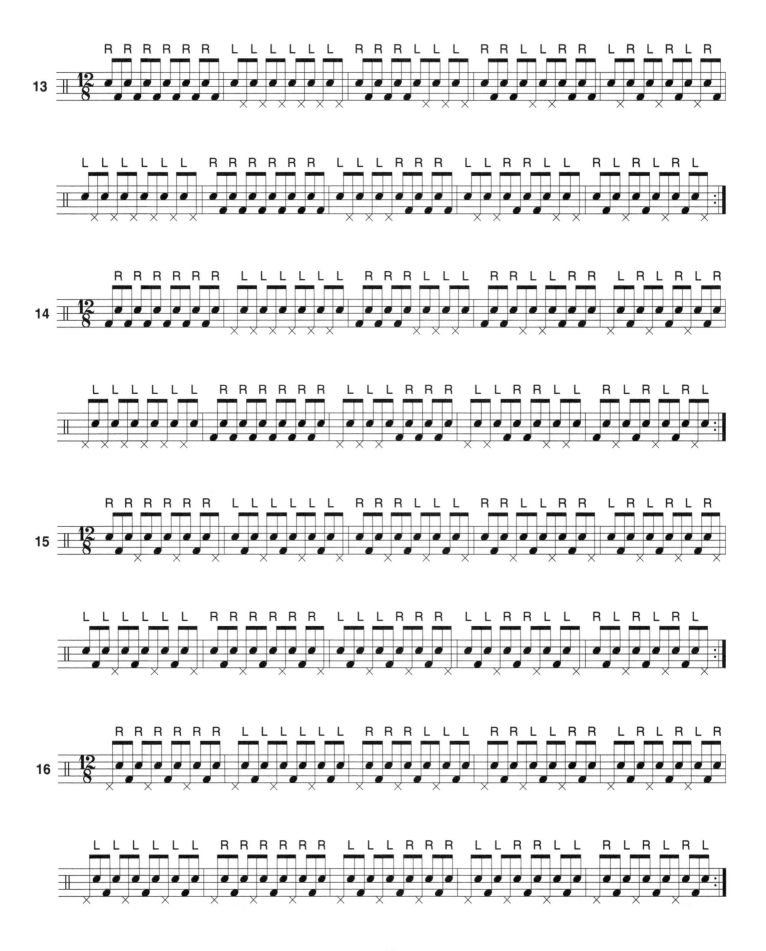

In Exercises 1–32, if you are not playing any hi-hat notes with the hands, tap quarter notes with the hi-hat pedal to achieve greater independence.

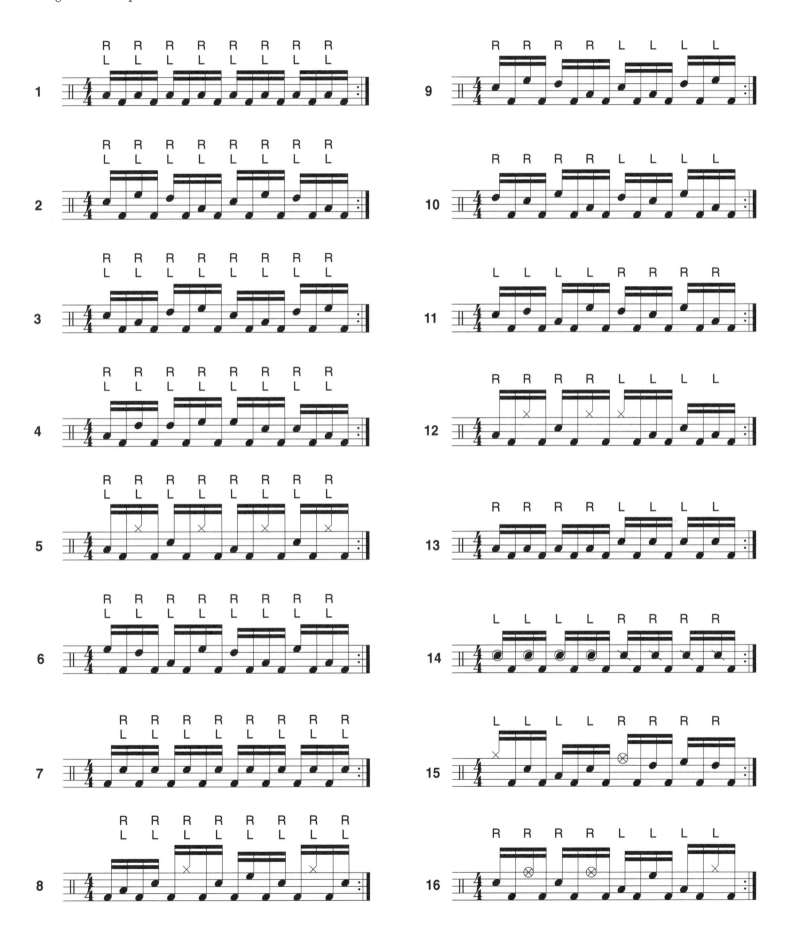

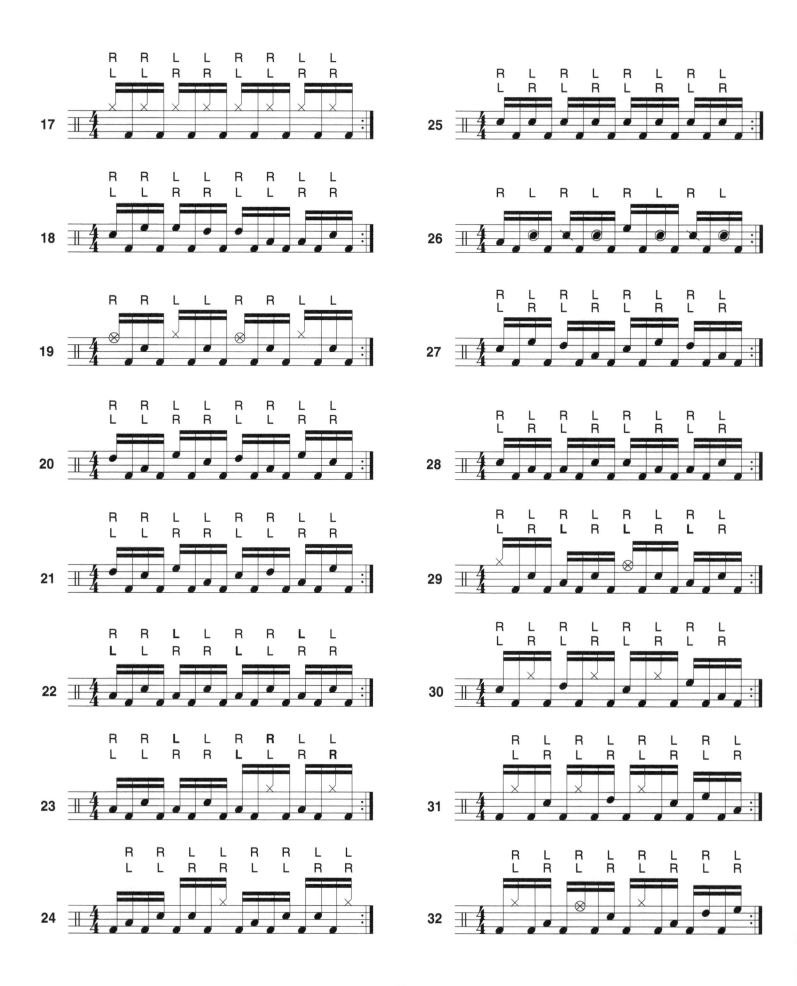

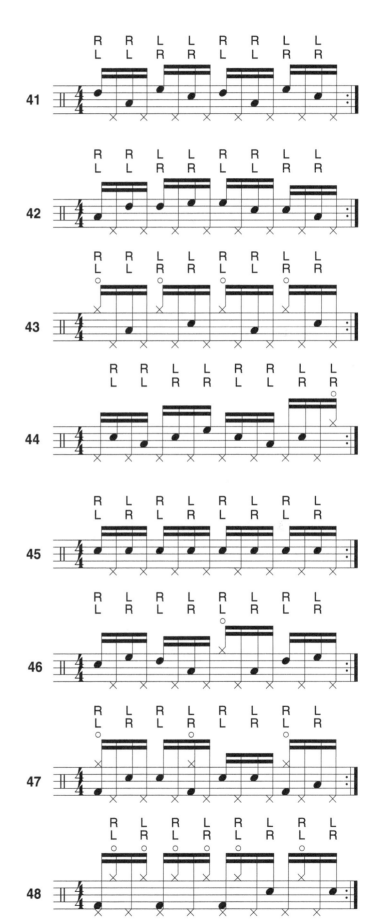

These exercises consist of two consecutive sixteenth notes on the bass drum. Try to give equal emphasis to both bass drum strokes as there is often a tendency to accent one or the other.

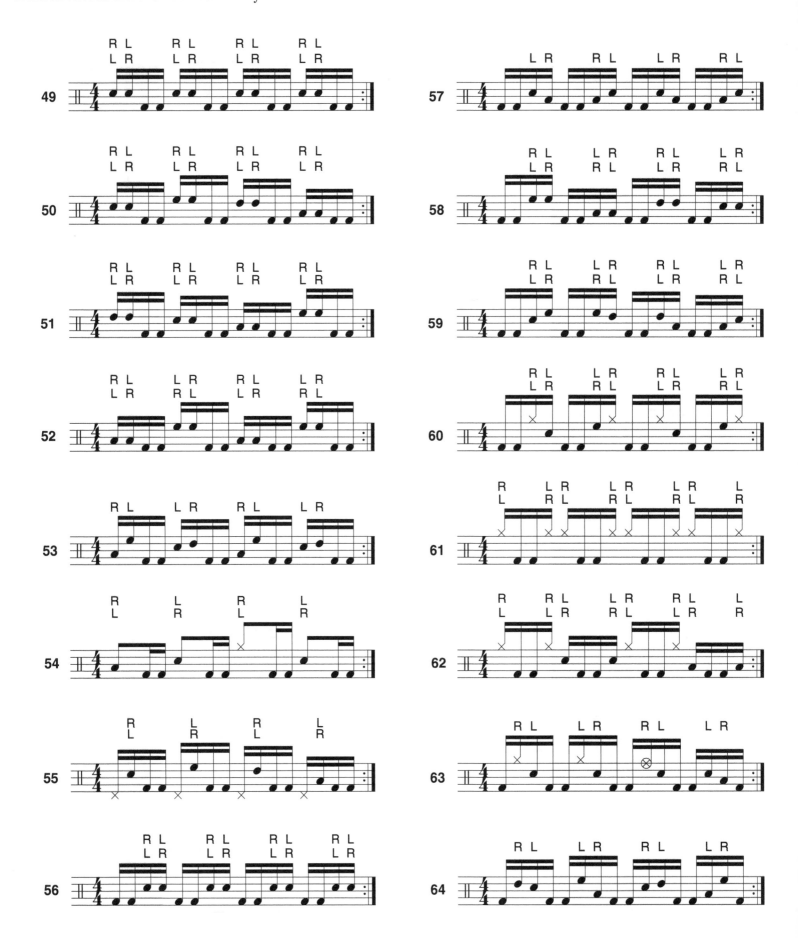

When striking two drums together in Exercise 67, use whatever sticking feels the most comfortable.

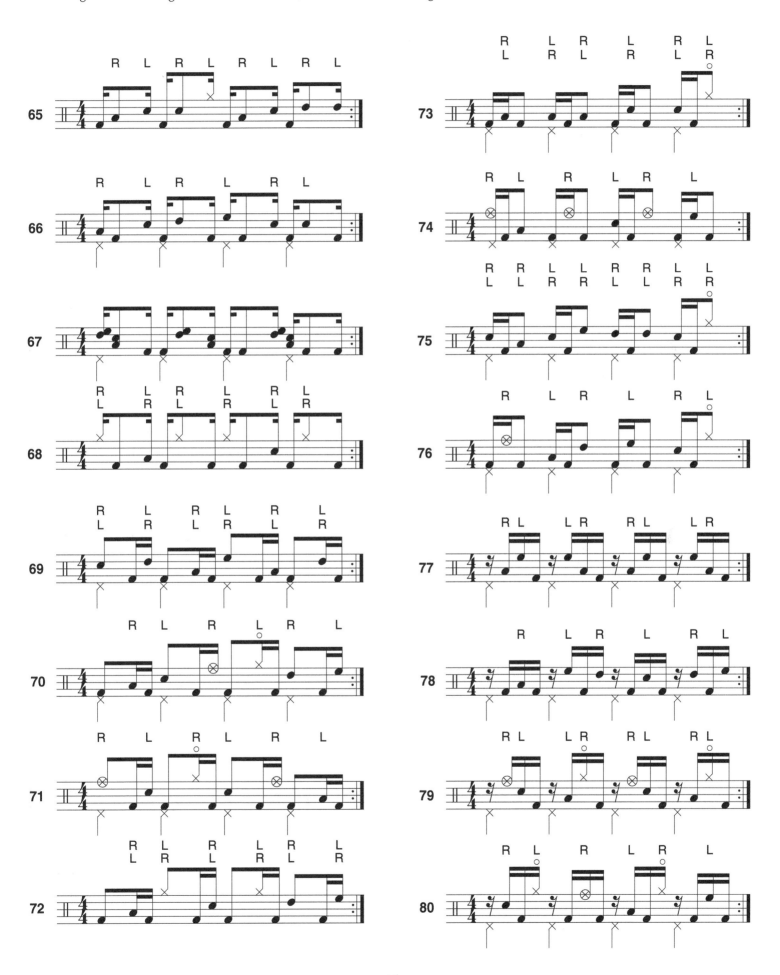

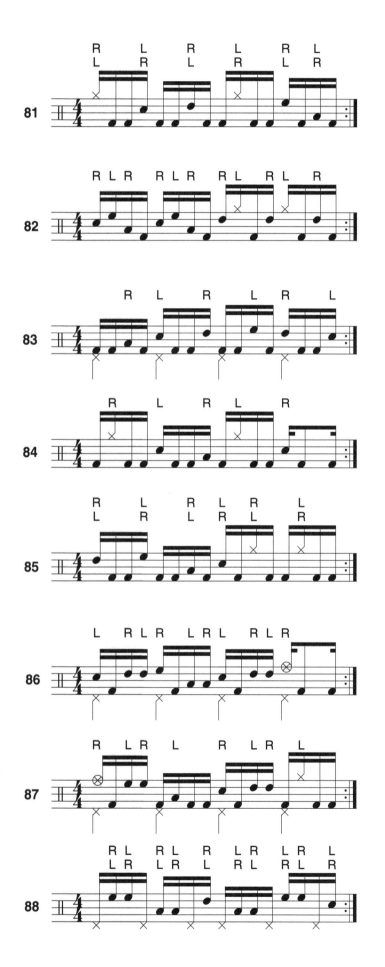

Make sure to follow the specified sticking patterns. Exercise 6 will sound more effective if the left-hand strokes are ghosted (played quietly). Try to play quarter notes with the hi-hat foot in exercises that do not include a hand stroke on the hi-hat.

1

2

3

4

5

6

7

8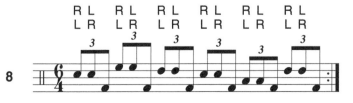

9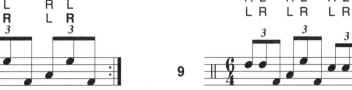

10

11

12

13

14

15

16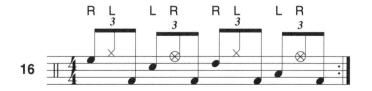

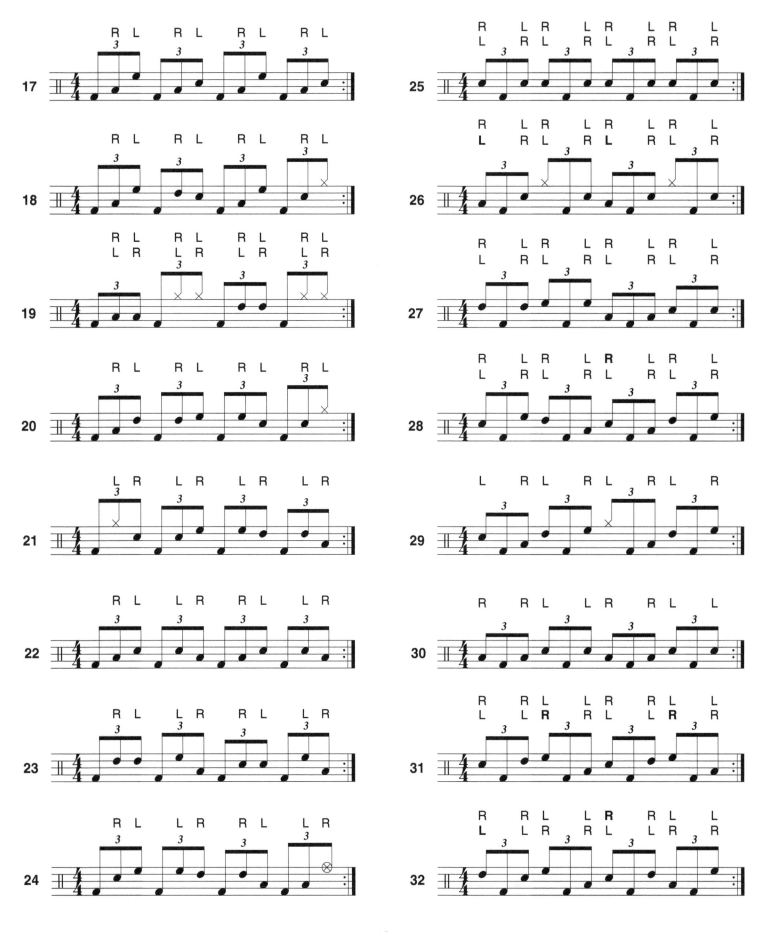

Sextuplets can be felt with a 2-note pulse or 3-note pulse. For this reason, each of the following eight patterns is represented with two different hi-hat foot patterns: (a) on the eighth note, defining a 2-note pulse, and (b) on every other sixteenth note (the eighth-note triplet), defining a 3-note pulse. These exercises can also be played with a quarter-note hi-hat pulse. It's a good idea to accent the quarter-note pulse, especially in Exercises 38a, 38b, 39a, and 39b.

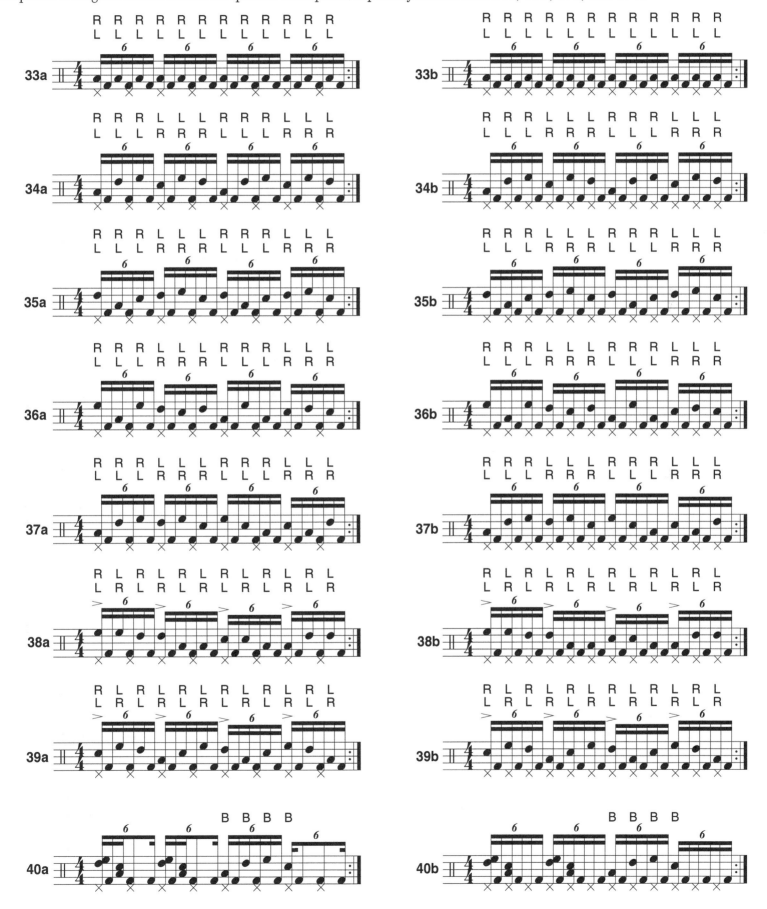

Continuing with triplet figures, the following patterns involve two consecutive notes on the bass drum. Try to give equal emphasis to both bass drum strokes as there is often a tendency to accent one or the other. As in previous exercises, try to keep a quarter-note pulse with the hi-hat foot in examples that do not include a hand stroke on the hi-hat.

With the exception of modern jazz drumming, the hi-hat pedal is most often used as a timekeeper. These exercises have been designed to strengthen the hi-hat foot's independence by having it play on some of the more syncopated parts of the beat.

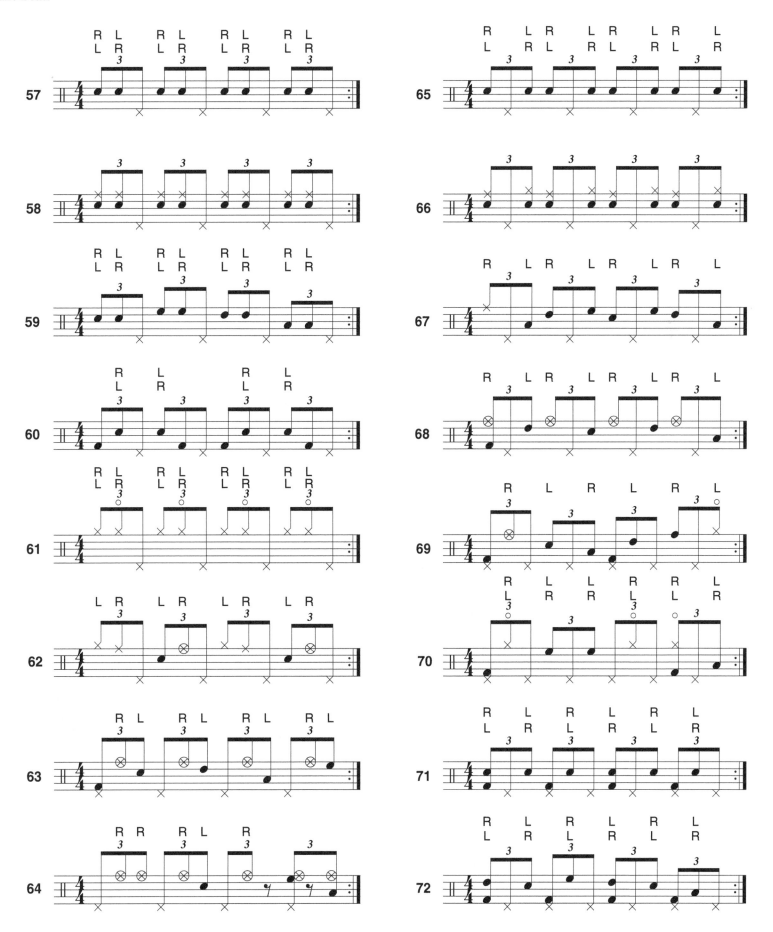

The ability to place accents anywhere desired, whether on the stronger parts of the beat or the more syncopated parts of the beat, is a tremendous asset to all styles of drumming. Keep a quarter-note pulse with either the hi-hat or bass drum to ensure that the accent is being placed correctly. For more impact, ghost the unaccented notes. In addition to improving coordination, these exercises will strengthen one's overall time concept.

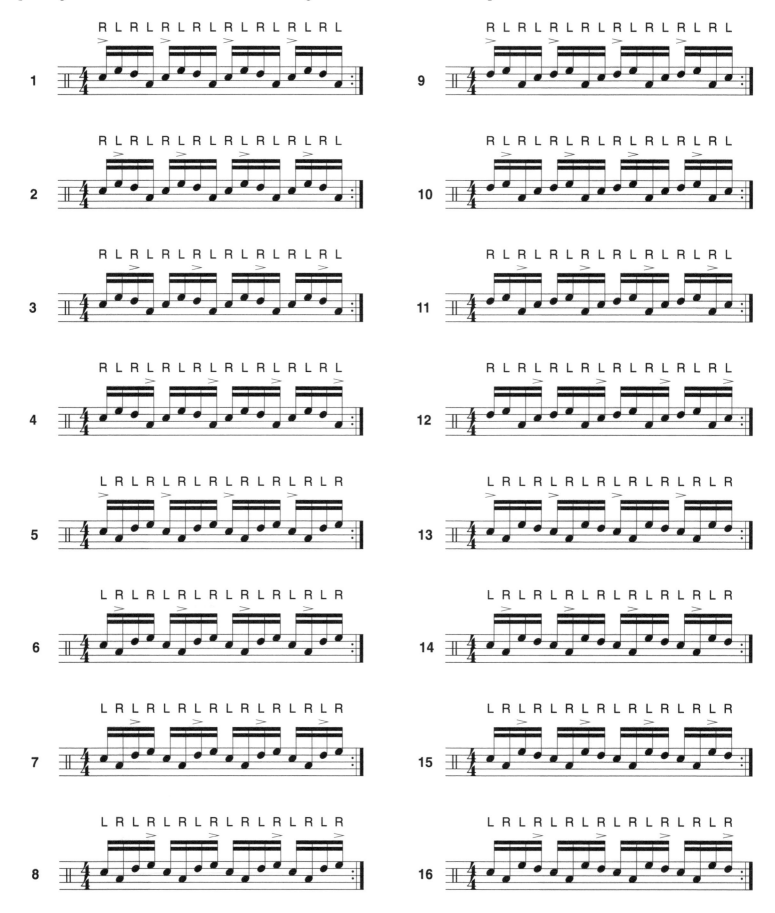

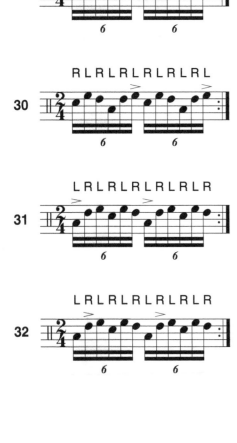
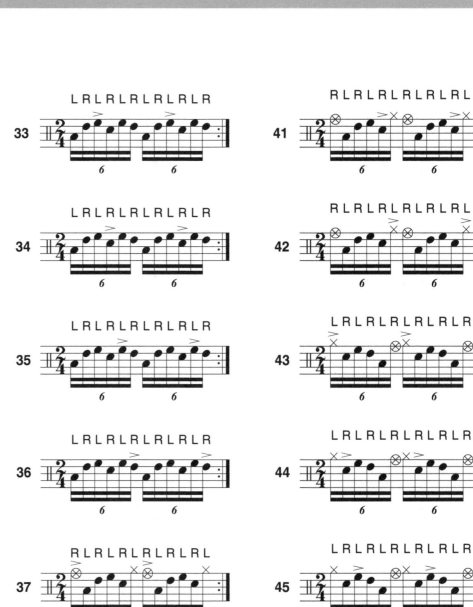
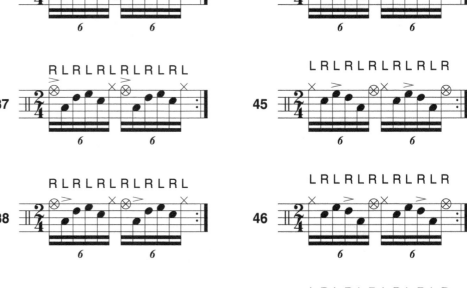
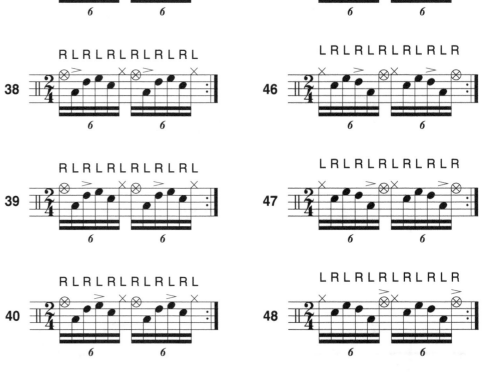

R L R L R L R L R L R L R L R L R L R L R L R L R L R L R L R L R L R L

49

R L R L R L R L R L R L R L R L R L R L R L R L R L R L R L R L R L R L

R L R L R L R L R L R L R L R L R L R L R L R L R L R L R L R L R L R L

50

L R L R L R L R L R L R L R L R L R L R L R L R L R L R L R L R L R L R

51

L R L R L R L R L R L R L R L R L R L R L R L R L R L R L R L R L R L R

L R L R L R L R L R L R L R L R L R L R L R L R L R L R L R L R L R L R

52

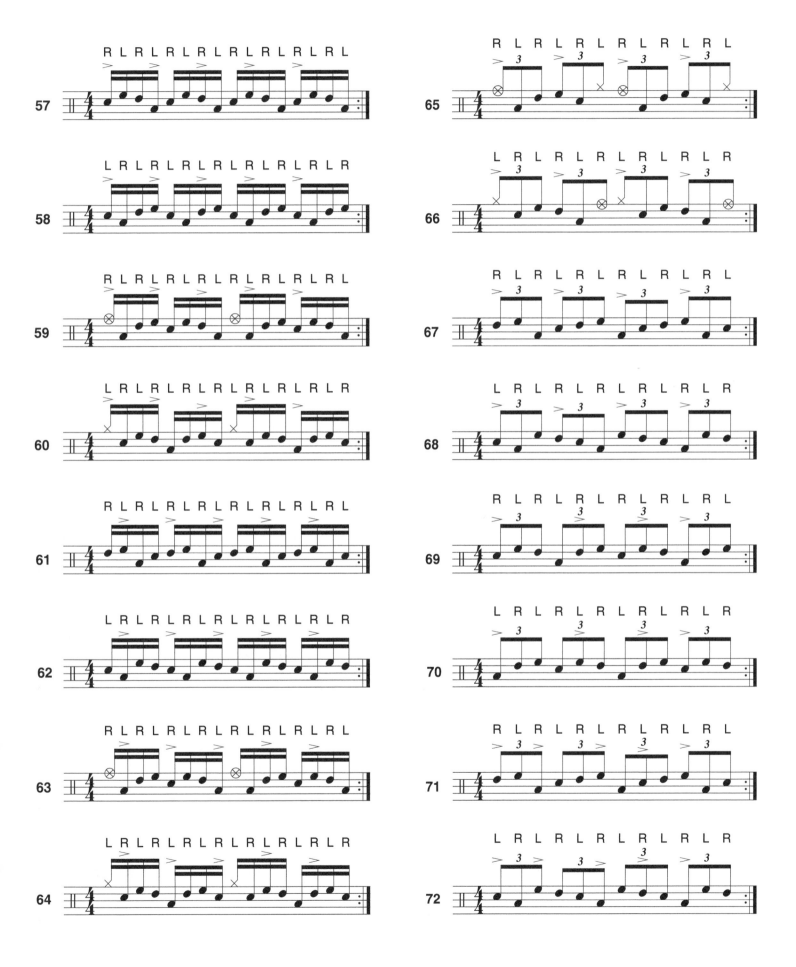

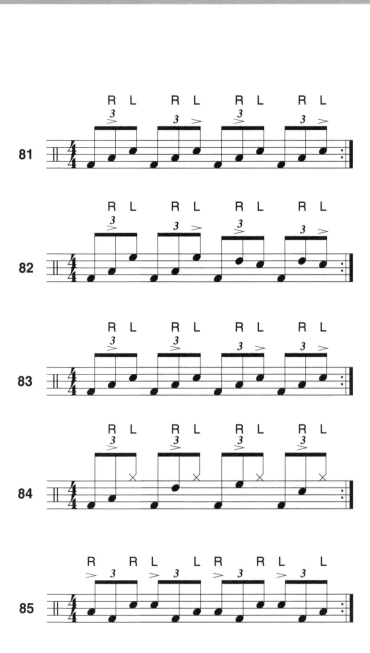

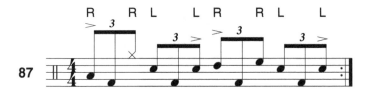
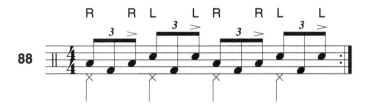

58

A solid, quick-snapping motion (predominantly on the snare but by no means limited to it) is extremely important in many styles of drumming including funk, fusion, and swing. Some of these grooves are complex and should be played slowly at first. Where stickings are not indicated, play cymbal or hi-hat with one hand and drums with the other.

LESSON
24

SUBJECT
Flam Rudiments

TECHNIQUE
Flams, Flam Taps, Flam Accents, Flam Paraddidles,
Swiss Triplets

Flam rudiments can provide unique sounds and textures on the drum set. Exercises 1–8 consist of Flams, Exercises 9–12 are Flam Taps, Exercises 13–16 are Flam Accents, Exercises 17–24 are Flam Paraddidles and Exercises 25–32 are Swiss Triplets. Be sure to place the grace note on the specified drum, as it is not always played on the same surface as the main stroke.

1

2

3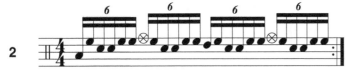

4

5

6

7

8

9

10

11

12

13

14

15

16

The arms will get a solid workout reaching for the various cymbals and hi-hat. Practice these exercises with and without the bass drum reinforcing the cymbal notes. If your setup includes two crashes, alternate between them in the examples that include two crash notes. When practicing for power, lay into the ride cymbal with the shoulder of the stick and go for a "sloshy" sound on the hi-hat.

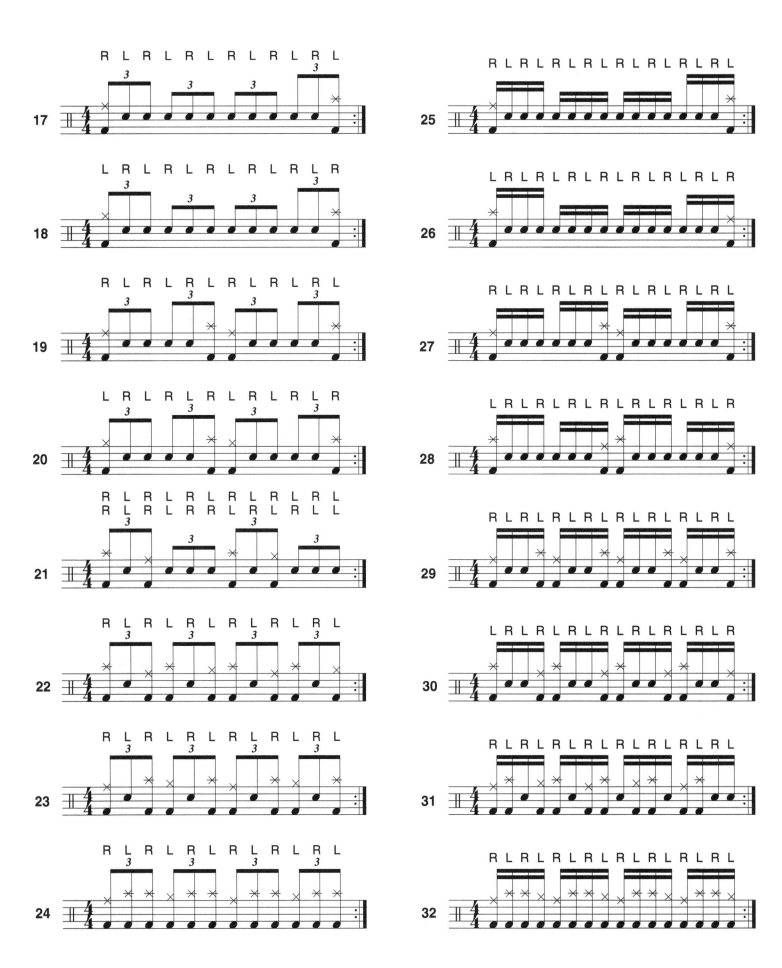

In addition to developing speed and power, the following exercises will be of tremendous help in strengthening the left side of the body. Every successive ride/crash/hi-hat stroke should be played with the opposite hand. Stickings above the notes refer to cymbals; stickings below the notes refer to drums.

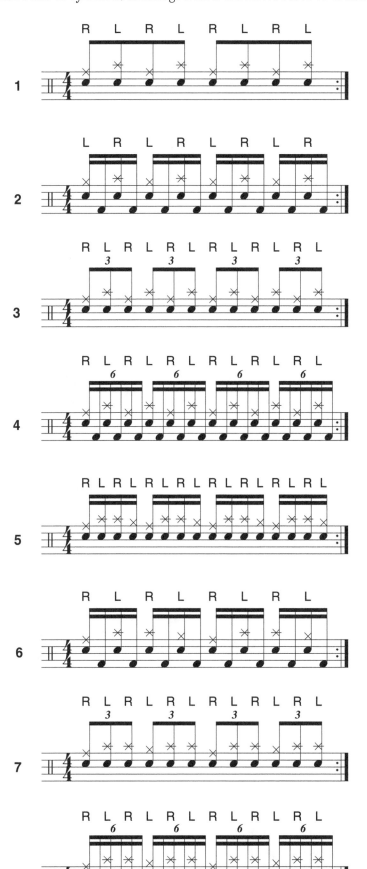

The rolls on this page should all be played as closed (multiple-bounce) rolls. Exercises 1 and 9, which each show the roll being played on a single surface, should be played on every sound surface in your drumset, as each surface has its own touch and feel and will require slight alterations to make the roll sound smooth and even. Keep time with quarter notes played very softly on the bass drum.

The following exercises combine closed (multiple-bounce) and open (double-stroke) rolls. Make sure to distinguish between the crisp, staccato, military sound of an open roll and the smooth, connected, concert sound of the closed roll. Play Exercises 17 and 23 on every drum and cymbal in the drum set.

Pay special attention to the stickings in the following exercises.

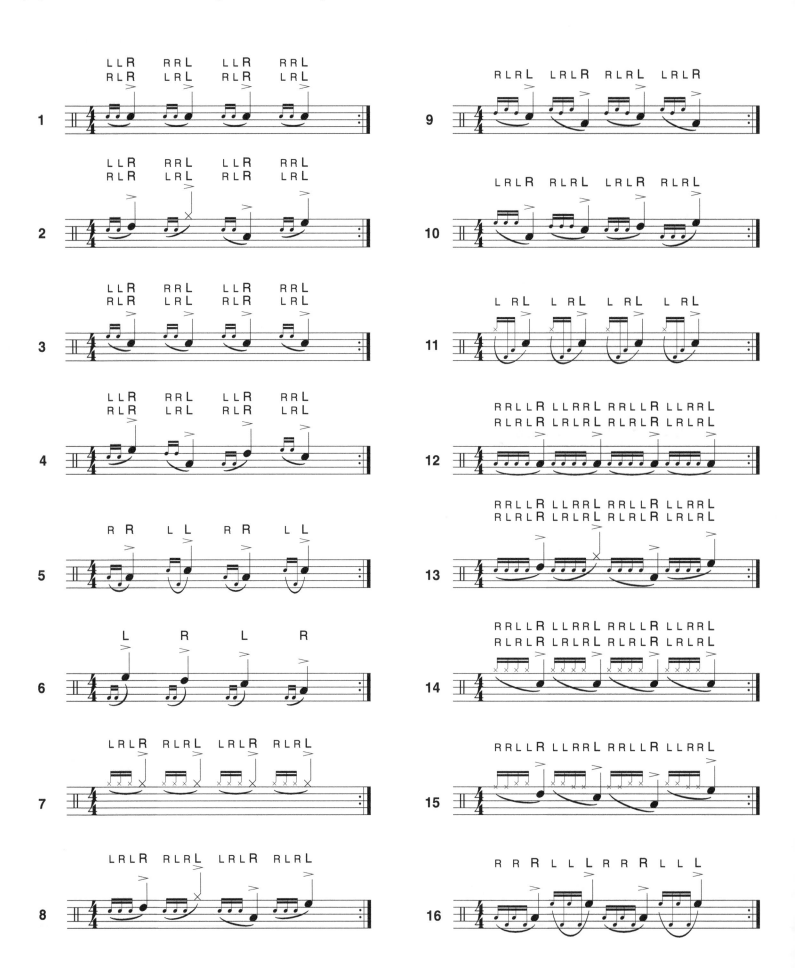

A useful technique involves playing both hands together with equal volume, either striking the same surface in unison or simultaneously striking two different surfaces. These are not the same as regular Flams in that there are no grace notes; each hand should play at the same volume and intensity level.

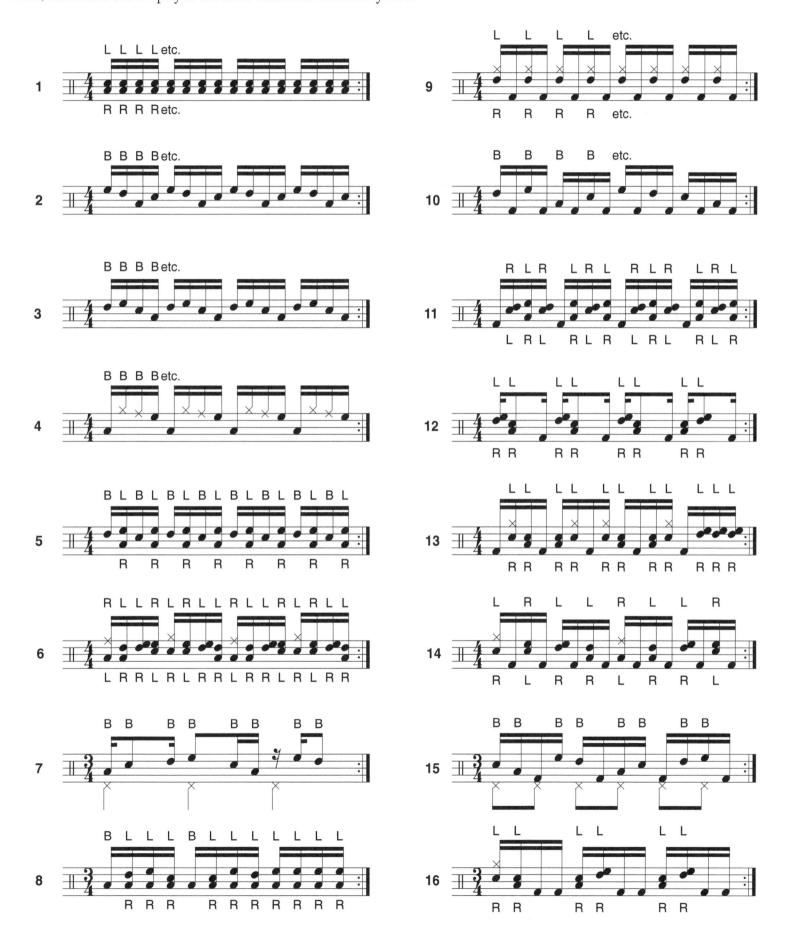

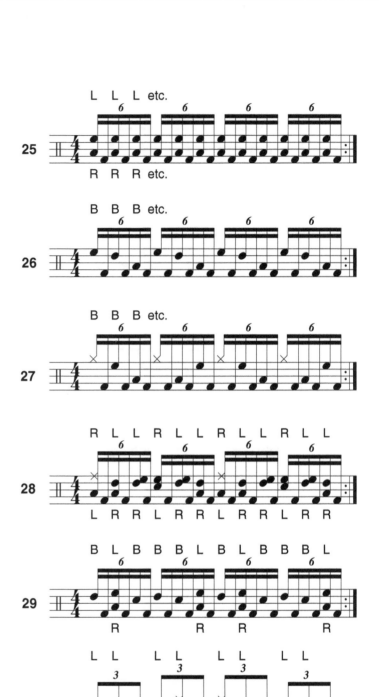

In the following exercises, one hand or pattern moves around the drum set in a clockwise motion and the other moves counterclockwise. It's almost as if one is a "mirror image" of the other.

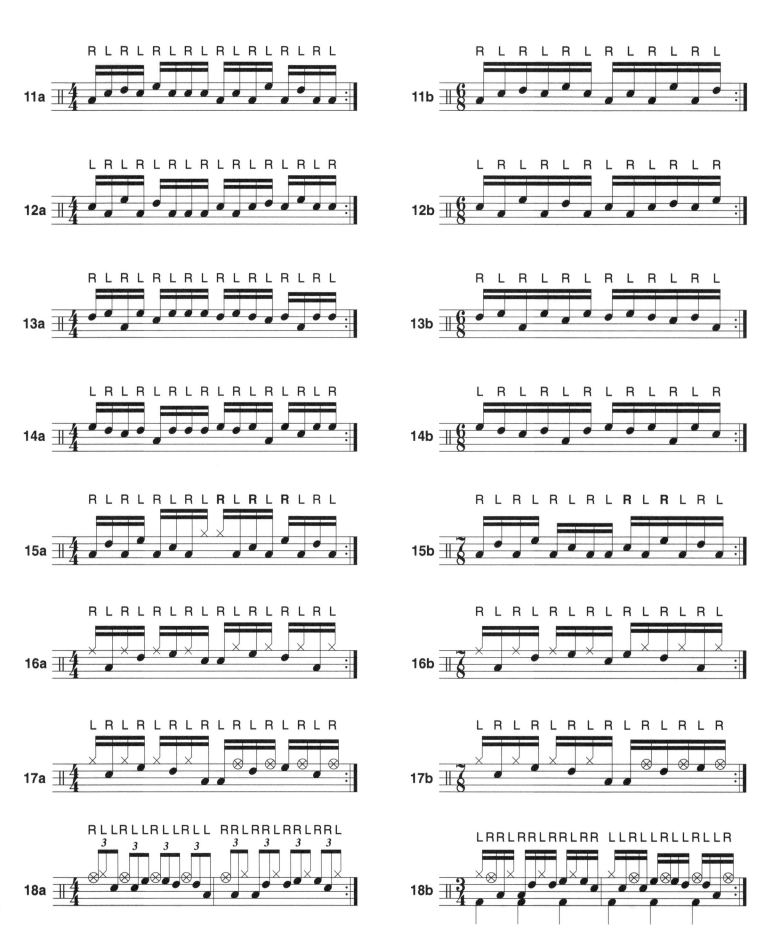

After you can play each pattern individually, combine the a and b versions of each exercise into a 2-bar pattern. Crossovers are indicated by stickings in **bold** type.

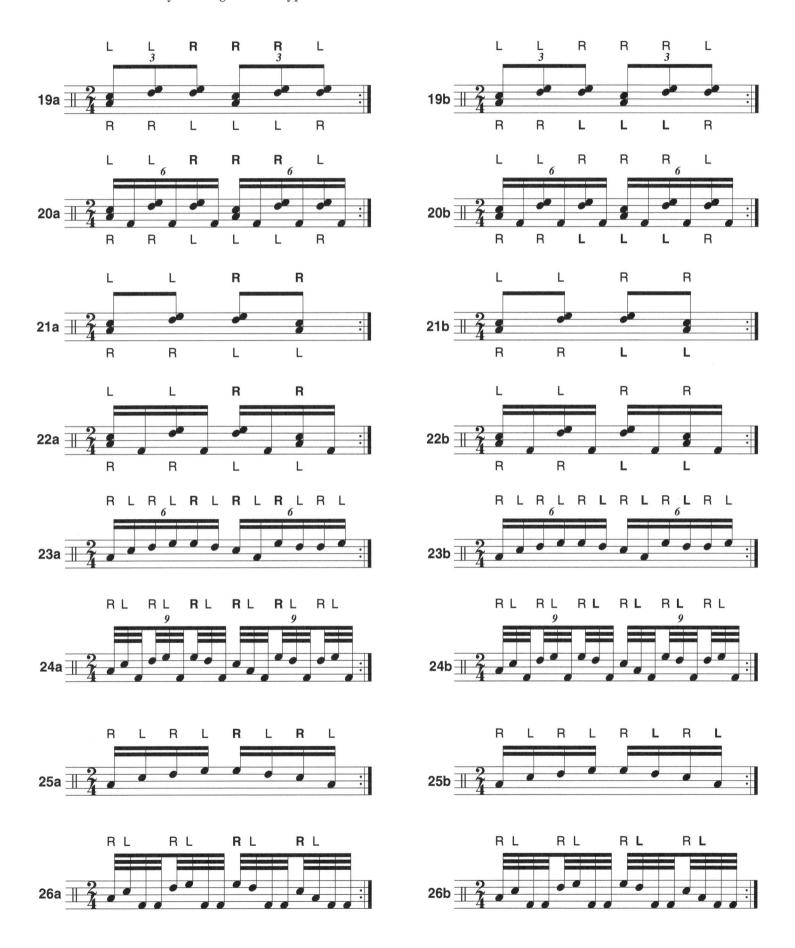

In column a, play each pattern with and without the notes in parenthesis.

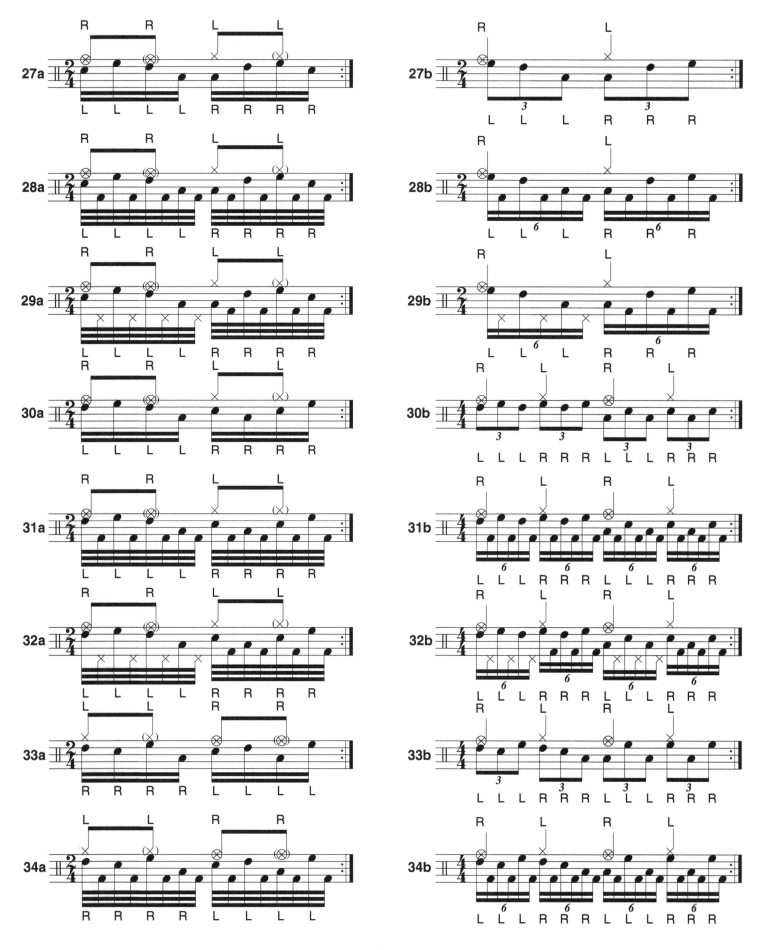

The exercises on this page feature patterns that use progressively fewer notes.

Crossovers can add visual excitement to a live performance. Like many of the exercises in this book, these examples put the hands, arms, and body through challenging, unusual, and somewhat uncomfortable motions in order to build greater command of the drum set. Follow the stickings carefully to ensure that both arms are receiving equal benefits from these exercises. The crossovers are indicated by **bold** type.

The patterns on this page show how a variety of exercises can be created from a single idea—in this case, Exercise 11 on page 76. The sky's the limit, so let your imagination fly. Note: Exercise 7 should be played as combination Flat Flams and press rolls.

1

2

3

4

5

6

7

8

9

10

11

12

13

14

15

We conclude with 2- and 4-measure combinations and variations of previous exercises, which provide a balanced work-out in and of themselves as they include techniques and patterns from throughout this text. As an added challenge, dynamic markings (including crescendos and decrescendos) accompany these exercises. Using dynamics adds a wider dimension and emotion to music. However, be sure you can play the patterns correctly before attempting to add the dynamic markings.

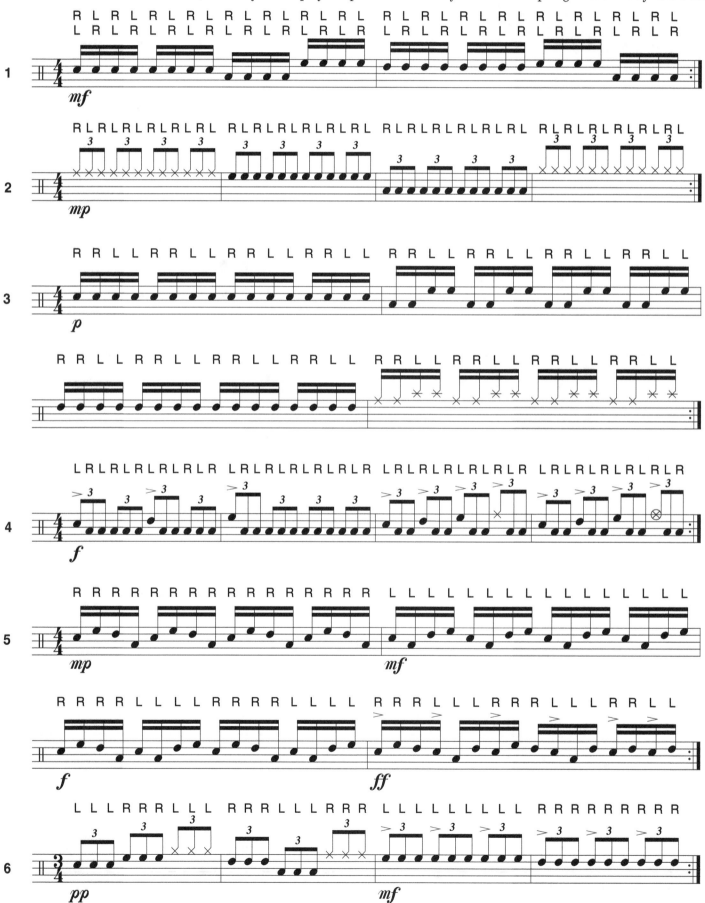

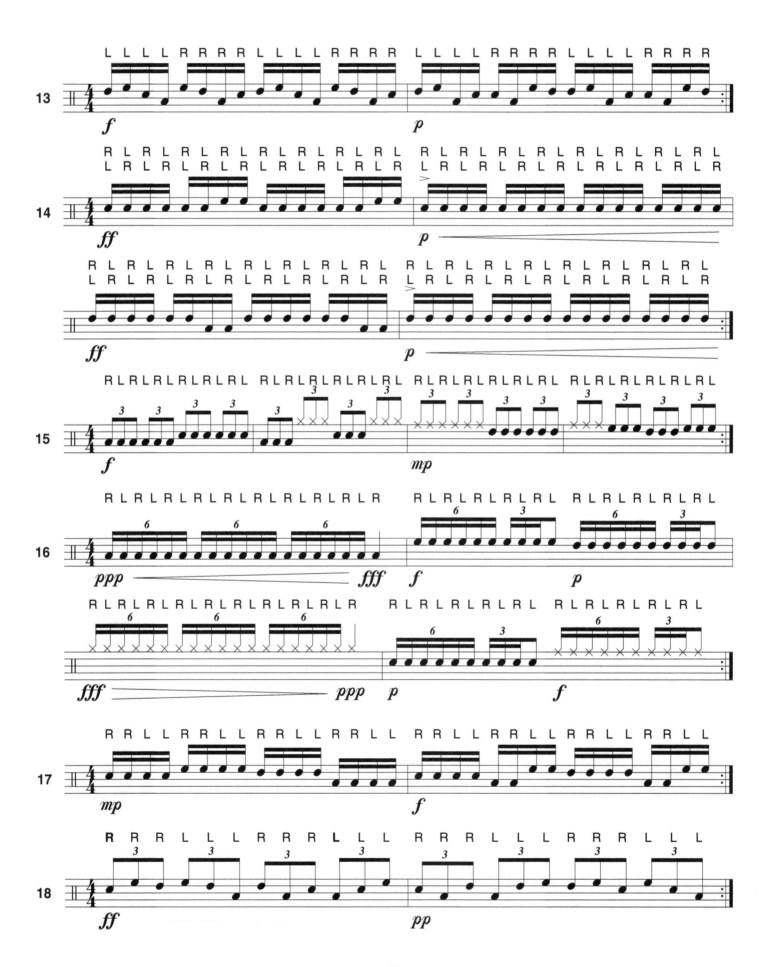

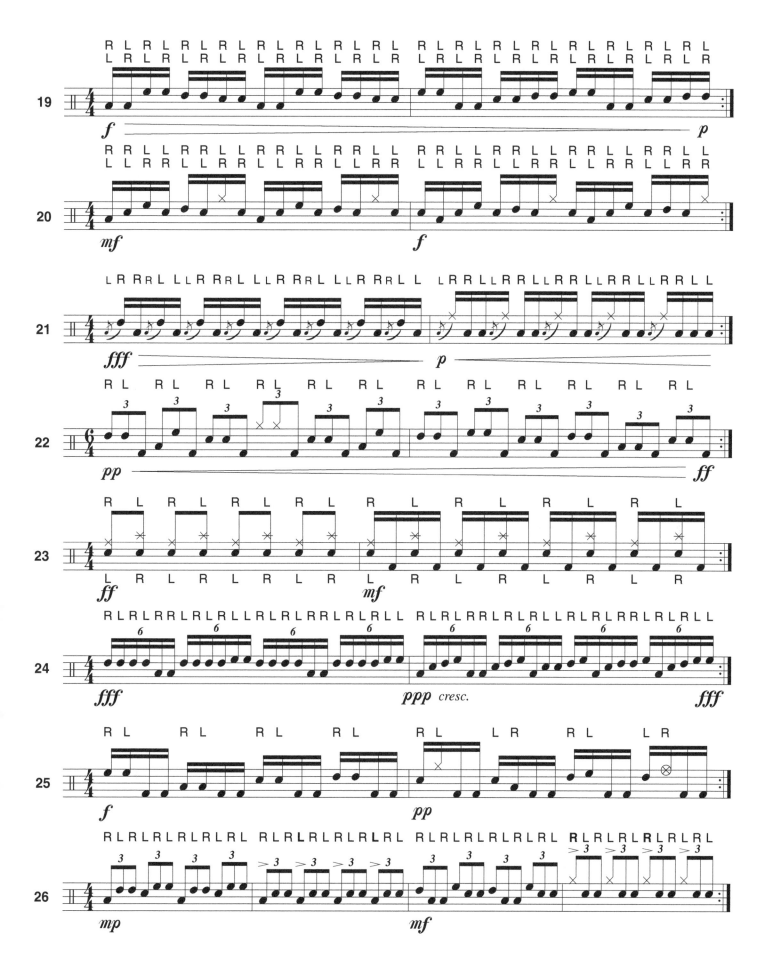

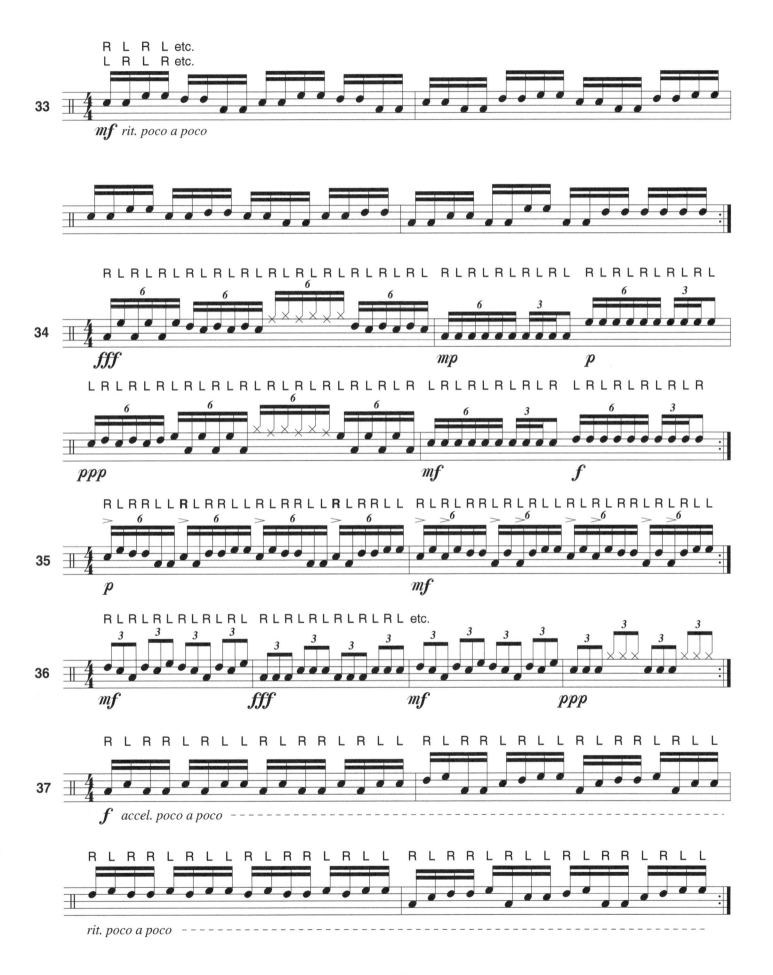

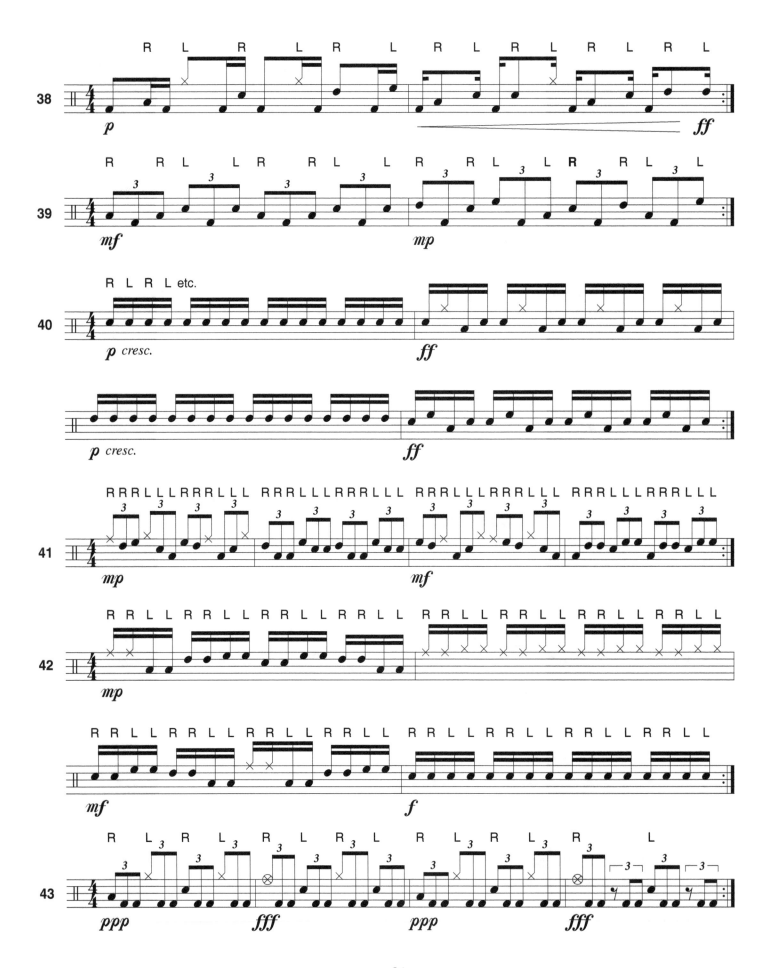

Exercises 48 and 49 can be played with various sticking ideas from Lessons 27, 30, and 32.

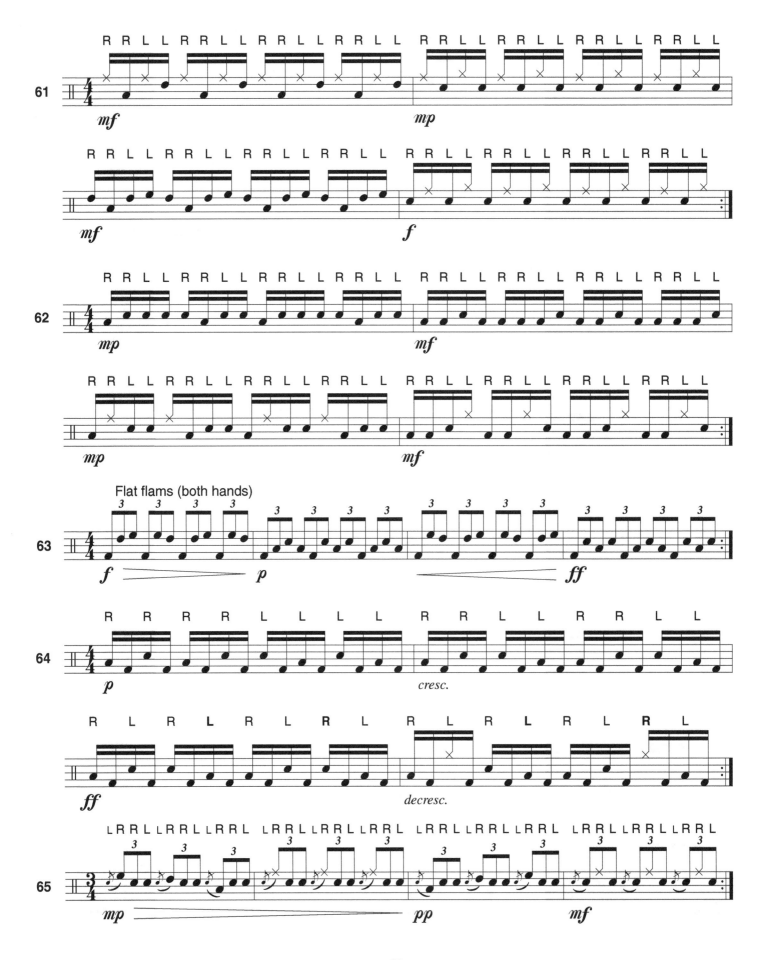

Rod Morgenstein is widely respected for his contributions to the world of drumming. He is a founding member of the ground-breaking progressive rock-fusion group the Dixie Dregs, who have received Grammy nominations for Best Rock Instrumental Performance for six of their recordings. The band, touted by *The Philadelphia Inquirer* as "possibly the most important, and certainly the most technically advanced instrumental group in progressive fusion," continues to record and tour. From 1983–86 Rod also recorded and toured with Dregs guitarist Steve Morse in the Steve Morse Band. Rod's unique style of drumming has earned him *Modern Drummer* magazine's Readers Poll award for Best Progressive Rock Drummer numerous times.

Rod is an original member of the heavy metal band Winger, whose recordings have reached gold and platinum status around the world. The band received an American Music Award nomination for Best New Heavy Metal Band in 1989. He has also recorded on solo projects by Kip Winger.

Other projects that Rod has been involved with include: the Rudess Morgenstein Project, a power duo featuring Rod and Dream Theater keyboardist Jordan Rudess; The Jelly Jam, which features Dream Theater bassist John Myung and King's X guitarist Ty Tabor; and jazz-fusion jam band Jazz Is Dead, which then featured bassist Alphonso Johnson, guitarist Jimmy Herring, and keyboardist T Lavitz. Rod was also part of a select group of drummers chosen to play on the Buddy Rich tribute CD, *Burning for Buddy*.

A graduate of the University of Miami (Florida) with a Bachelor of Music degree, Rod is very involved in drum education. He has performed at hundreds of clinics and drum festivals around the world. He authored the audio cassette/book packages *Grooving In Styles/Filling In the Holes*, and *Double Bass Drumming* (Cherry Lane), the instructional video *Putting It All Together* (Warner Bros.), and co-authored with Rick Mattingly the book/CD package *The Drumset Musician* (Hal Leonard). He has also been a columnist for *Modern Drummer*, *Rhythm* (UK), and *Sticks* (Germany) magazines. Rod also authored and teaches the online course *Rock Drums* through Berkleemusic.com, the continuing education division of Berklee College of Music.

Rod is a Professor of Percussion at Berklee College of Music in Boston.

Dynamic Drum Publications from Berklee Press

BOOKS	DVDS

BERKLEE INSTANT DRUM SET
by Ron Savage
This book/CD pack teaches first-time drummers rock, funk, and jazz beats within minutes. Features an accompanying CD so you can jam with the band in a variety of musical styles.
50449513 Book/CD Pack $17.99

BERKLEE PRACTICE METHOD: DRUM SET
by Ron Savage, Casey Scheuerell and the Berklee Faculty
This sensational series lets you improve your intuitive sense of timing and improvisation, develop your technique and reading ability, and master your role in the groove.
50449429 Book/CD Pack $14.95

BEYOND THE BACKBEAT:
FROM ROCK & FUNK TO JAZZ & LATIN
by Larry Finn
Learn how to take any basic rock/funk drum beat and morph it into jazz and world music feels. Improve your chops, expand your versatility, and develop your own style.
50449447 Book/CD Pack $19.95

DOUBLE-BASS DRUM INTEGRATION
These timetables and other road-tested exercises methodically introduce double pedal patterns into your beats, helping you play them intuitively, revealing the possibilities of double bass drums.
00120208 Book/Online Audio $19.99

DRUM SET WARM-UPS
by Rod Morgenstein
Legendary drummer Rod Morgenstein reveals his innovative warm-up method designed to limber up your entire body.
50449465 Book $12.99

DRUM STUDIES
by Dave Vose
These studies will help you to master a broad range of techniques and integrate them into your playing so that you can achieve greater depth in your grooves and general precision in all your drumming.
50449617 Book $12.99

THE READING DRUMMER – SECOND EDITION
by Dave Vose
Features: more than 50 lessons complete with general practice tips; steady learning progression from reading quarter notes to 16th-note triplets; and more.
50449458 Book $14.99

LEARNING TO LISTEN:
THE JAZZ JOURNEY OF GARY BURTON
by Gary Burton
Gary Burton shares his 50 years of experiences at the top of the jazz scene.
00117798 Book $27.99

MASTERING THE ART OF BRUSHES
by Jon Hazilla
This in-depth workshop, complete with helpful diagrams practice audio, features 10 essential concepts, 32 brush patterns, rhythm table exercises, and more.
50449459 Book/Online Audio $19.99

PHRASING: ADVANCED RUDIMENTS FOR
CREATIVE DRUMMING
by Russ Gold
Phrasing will help you expand your vocabulary using standard rudiments and exciting rhythmic concepts, making your playing more conversational, dynamic, and focused.
00120209 Book $19.99

EIGHT ESSENTIALS OF DRUMMING
by Ron Savage
Become a well-rounded drummer with sound technique, solid time, and expressive musicianship by mastering these eight essentials.
50448048 Book/CD Pack $19.99

READING STUDIES FOR DRUMS AND PERCUSSION
by Ron Delp
These exercises will help musicians move between instruments more accurately, while enhancing their reading ability for recording work, shows, and the theater pit.
50449550 Book $9.99

RUDIMENT GROOVES FOR DRUM SET
by Rick Considine
Discover how rudiments become the foundation for all grooves and moves, including: single and double strokes; stroked rolls; drags; flams; and more.
50448001 Book/Online Audio $19.95

STICKINGS & ORCHESTRATIONS FOR DRUM SET
by Casey Scheuerell
Technical explanations and extensive practice exercises with the play-along audio will help you make your fills become more vibrant and your solos more virtuosic.
50448049 Book/Online Audio $22.99

WORLD JAZZ DRUMMING
by Mark Walker
This book/CD pack teaches you how to: incorporate world instruments into a standard drum kit; coordinate stick, foot, hand techniques to enrich your palette of articulations; and more.
50449568 Book/CD Pack $22.99

BASIC AFRO-CUBAN RHYTHMS FOR
DRUM SET AND HAND PERCUSSION
featuring Ricardo Monzón
Learn how to play and practice the classic rhythms of the Afro-Cuban tradition with Berklee professor Ricardo Monzón. 55 minutes.
50448012 DVD $19.95

BEGINNING DJEMBE
by Michael Markus & Joe Galeota
This hands-on workshop will help you produce a good sound, develop a healthy playing technique, and learn the essential concepts and rhythms of West African djembe drumming. 1 hr., 36 minutes
50449639 DVD $14.99

CREATIVE JAZZ IMPROVISATION
FOR DRUM SET
Featuring Yoron Israel
Yoron Israel will help you to enhance your improvisational language and lead you to more musical, concise and dynamic drum set solos and comping. 51 minutes.
50449549 DVD $24.95

KENWOOD DENNARD:
THE STUDIO/TOURING DRUMMER
Dennard teaches how to: get the most out of every practice session, internalize the melody, play melodic solos, and more! 61 minutes.
50448034 DVD $19.95

NEW WORLD DRUMMING
by Pablo Peña "Pablitodrum"
Learn to: Play drum set in a percussion ensemble, incorporate world rhythms and sounds into a standard drum kit, create drum parts that are appropriate to the style and ensemble, and more. 41 minutes.
50449547 DVD $24.95

0319
379

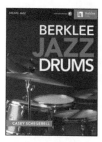
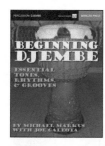

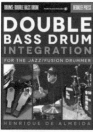

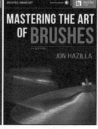

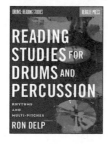